Adult education at the Council of Europe – Challenging the future

(1960–93)

Gérald Bogard

Council for Cultural Co-operation

Council of Europe Press, 1994

French edition:
L'éducation des adultes – Un pari progressiste du Conseil de l'Europe
ISBN 92-871-2486-8

The opinions expressed in this work are those of the author(s) and do not necessarily reflect the official policy of the Council for Cultural Co-operation of the Council of Europe.

All correspondence concerning this publication or the reproduction or translation of all or part of the document should be addressed to the Director of Education, Culture and Sport of the Council of Europe (F-67075 Strasbourg Cedex).

Publishing and Documentation Service
Council of Europe
F-67075 Strasbourg Cedex

ISBN 92-871-2487-6
© Council of Europe, 1994
Printed in the Netherlands

The **Council of Europe** was founded in 1949 to achieve greater unity between European parliamentary democracies. It is the oldest of the European political institutions and has thirty-two member states,[1] including the twelve members of the European Community. It is the widest intergovernmental and interparliamentary grouping in Europe, and has its headquarters in the French city of Strasbourg.

Only questions related to national defence are excluded from the Council of Europe's work, and the Organisation has activities in the following areas: democracy, human rights and fundamental freedoms; media and communication; social and economic affairs; education, culture, heritage and sport; youth; health; environment and regional planning; local democracy and legal co-operation.

The **European Cultural Convention** was opened for signature in 1954. This international treaty is open to European countries that are not members of the Council of Europe, and it enables them to take part in the Organisation's programmes on education, culture, sport and youth. So far, thirty-eight states have acceded to the European Cultural Convention: the Council of Europe's thirty-two member states plus Albania, Belarus, Croatia, the Holy See, Latvia and the Russian Federation.

The **Council for Cultural Co-operation (the CDCC)** is responsible for the Council of Europe's work on education, culture and sport. Four specialised committees — the Education Committee, the Standing Conference on University Problems, the Culture Committee and the Cultural Heritage Committee — help the CDCC to carry out its tasks under the European Cultural Convention. There is

---

1. Austria, Belgium, Bulgaria, Cyprus, Czech Republic, Denmark, Estonia, Finland, France, Germany, Greece, Hungary, Iceland, Ireland, Italy, Liechtenstein, Lithuania, Luxembourg, Malta, Netherlands, Norway, Poland, Portugal, Romania, San Marino, Slovak Republic, Slovenia, Spain, Sweden, Switzerland, Turkey, United Kingdom.

also a close working relationship between the CDCC and the regular conferences of specialised European ministers responsible for education, for culture and for the cultural heritage.

The CDCC's programmes are an integral part of the Council of Europe's work and, like the programmes in other sectors, they contribute to the Organisation's three overriding policy objectives for the 1990s:

- the protection, reinforcement and promotion of human rights and fundamental freedoms and pluralist democracy;

- the promotion of an awareness of European identity;

- the search for common responses to the great challenges facing European society.

The CDCC's education programme covers school, higher and adult education, as well as educational research. At present, its main priorities are projects on the European dimension of secondary education, university co-operation, adult education and social change, modern languages, and the pooling of results of educational research.

Contents

Progress, crisis, change

The 1980s were above all years of increasing social marginalisation. In Europe, the numbers of poor and unemployed ran into millions. Several million job-seekers, a large proportion of them confused young people and women finding it difficult to gain access to the job market, not to mention those "excluded" from industry, the under-educated and under-qualified, who were the first to be affected — and for the longest time — by the transformation of the conditions of production and the new job requirements. The major difficulties facing them were the decline in their living conditions, an emotional deficit, loss of self-esteem and therefore self-confidence, and also lack of a future. They were the "non-public of education".

In the west as in the east, where, as we know, the reconstruction of systems in the social, economic, political and cultural fields will be slow, politicians have fallen back, in this situation of emergency, on mechanisms and principles which are not equal to the task. As they feel their way forward, the slow task of mutual rediscovery is beginning between politicians and educators on the ground.

Today, the crisis in education cannot be understood without reference to the crisis of democracy (which is in jeopardy in the west and still remains to be constructed in the east) underlying it. And how could things be otherwise, when democracy and education have been interlinked since the first democratic regimes emerged? Every citizen, to qualify as such, needs to be educated.

Although the Party-States have collapsed in the east, the Nation-States in the west are hard put to know where they belong: everywhere, the emergence of the demands of minorities and supra-national entities are destabilising factors for them.

In the face of recent scientific and technological developments, man's former preconceptions are marking time, faced as they are with a plurality of fragmentary approaches, which point up the defects in existing legal or ethical systems. The gradual integration of the world economy and the restructuring of production systems call for new skills, whereas persistent unemployment and poverty highlight the crippling shortcomings in education. The social regulatory mechanisms which formerly guaranteed the major social equilibria now make for only imperfect social cohesion. The systems for the socialisation of individuals, hitherto based on organising people's lives into three age-groups and on a "division of labour" between basic education and vocational training, are now revealing their unsuitability.

In this context, adult education, as practiced on the ground against a mixed array of social demands, is now more than ever thrust into the centre of the debate. So it is useful to recall its origins.

From 1962 to 1966, the aim was to harmonise education systems. Yet this endeavour was never carried through. Despite the democratisation of education, the reduction of inequalities has been much less than originally hoped. The necessity therefore emerged for a "global and fundamentally new concept, integrating all forms of education and capable of responding to the growing and diversified needs of each individual".

Two different, and equally radical, ideas then emerge. The first is that of *"descolarisation"*. Ivan Illich used the term to denounce the belief in education as a system at the service of equality and the free development of the individual. Being parts of the system, schools are to be eliminated in order to liberate the individual, thus giving him an opportunity to change society. The second idea, that of *permanent education*, professes to be just as complete, just as systematic, but less marked by ideology. If the liberating technologies in which Illich vested such hope are to be placed wholly at the disposal of the individual, then the user must be master of his social environment. Social relations alone are the determining factor.

The idea of permanent education was to fall on fertile ground at the Council of Europe, where the protection and promotion of human rights as well as of pluralist democracy occupy a prominent place. It performs the role of analyst, at the same time as being an aim in itself. Education, universally regarded as necessary to the exercise of citizenship, is still unequally shared. Everywhere, women and men are prevented from gaining access to it and thereby attaining what it makes possible, namely a career, personal development, independence, etc. Not only is this a violation — or at least an infringement — of one of the human rights; those affected are also denied the complete exercise of the other components of these rights. These conditions have together led to the development of a rich programme of activities in the Council of Europe's Out-of-School Education Division.

Nowadays, training enjoys a consensus. In many countries, legislation gives adults the right to training; there are various forms of financial aid; there are facilities, for which the demand increases by the day. However, there is no talk of permanent education having triumphed. It had other ambitions. It aimed to be a "system of systems", aspired to serve as a lever for overthrowing school systems regarded as unsuitable and segregatory.

What was done was mostly outside school, and exerted little influence on it. Above all, the 1970s saw the triumph of vocational training. A genuine institutional innovation of the crisis years, it is one of the most promising areas of the Europe of the Community and the Europe of social dialogue. But although an ever-increasing number of workers have benefited from it, it has only become a "right" for workers in gainful employment; for those excluded from work, it has remained a second-best version of its counterpart, a "duty to be occupied".

The time for these social projects which a modernist ideology devised at the watershed of the 1970s is past. The *leitmotif* of a crisis, strongly present throughout the Council's Project No. 9, and which in that project was to capitalise on the theme of community development, is gradually being replaced by the idea of social change. It seems somewhat improbable that, to use the phrase coined by Bertrand Schwartz, the tendency to provide "yet more of the same" can persist. The time has therefore come to contemplate a new role and a new place for education and, in particular, for adult education.

Our era belongs — and can only belong — to the surveyor. Among the changes we see, there are some that are structurally decisive. It is the task of the educator to plan the terrain, with the preservation of democracy as the horizon and, as the immediate goal, the individual in whatever relationship he can sustain with the many networks that constitute the reality of the present-day social fabric.

**First stage
Permanent education (1970-80):
adapting man to change
and modernising society**

Permanent education, the improbable adventure

I. The Europe of the Council in the 1950s and 1960s

A new socio-economic landscape

The second world war displaced nearly 30 million people. National economies were in ruins. Industrial production had halved since 1939. Agricultural production had fallen by one third in western Europe. At the end of 1949 Europe was divided into two economic, political, ideological and military blocs, each linked to one of the two superpowers which had emerged victorious from the war. Yet this did not prevent the construction of Europe from becoming one of the great post-war adventures, with the birth of a number of institutions, foremost among them being the Council of Europe and the Atlantic Pact.

From the 1950s to the mid-1970s, Europe enjoyed exceptional growth, helped by the restoration of sound currencies, a newly dynamic demography, and also by the action of governments, espousing the theories of Keynes in support of economic growth.

The first image which comes to mind from that period is of the strong post-war birth-rate despite high mortality (11%). The resulting net demographic rejuvenation constituted a major growth factor. The other dominant image is of urbanisation. While rural communities were emptied of a proportion of their inhabitants, the "old continent" was swept by house-building fever: "large housing estates" and "new towns" bore witness, together with the fantastic development of communications, to the boundless expansion in lifestyles and human behaviour taking place. Lastly, the drawing-in of huge numbers of workers

15

made available by the new wave of rural exodus, and of foreign workers, led to an extraordinary mixing of populations.

The 1960s were also the years of technology. Its formidable progress led to substantial productivity gains, enabling production to grow faster than the size of the workforce. The forward march of the United States gradually spread through Europe, step-by-step with the proliferation of multinational companies and technology transfers. Until the mid-1960s, European countries made an unprecedented effort to carry research forward, devoting some 20% of their national income to the creation of capital equipment and acquiring a modern industrial base.

The prime field of innovation, industry, grew very fast in the 1950s, slowing down slightly in the following decade. From 1960 onwards, the "advanced" industries, stimulated by military orders from governments and developing the most advanced technologies — nuclear, aerospace and electronics — took over the lead from the sectors geared to family consumption. This *second industrial revolution* upset the existing balances, to the detriment of the former industries (textiles, iron and steel, shipbuilding) which were finding it difficult to modernise. Because of this, sectoral disparities were compounded by strong national and regional disparities. Until the mid-1970s, growth and the technological progress which accompanied it profoundly altered the nature of work and the distribution of the workforce. The pattern of stable employment established itself under the combined effect of economic concentration and the increase in the number of wage-earners. Whereas after 1945, European agriculture suffered a decline symbolised by the acceleration of the rural exodus,[1] industrial jobs for technicians and "white-collar" workers increased spectacularly while the numbers

---

1. The peasantry now represented only a very small fraction of the working population in western Europe.

of "blue-collar" workers, "metal bashers", foundry workers and miners, the engines of the preceding industrial generation, diminished. This was less a matter of homogenisation of the worker's lot than a displacement and a redefinition of differences: heavy, dangerous jobs had not disappeared from the industrial world; it was just that they had increasingly been taken over by the successive waves of an immigrant sub-proletariat; nor was soul-destroying production line work eradicated.

The change in living environments

The welfare state and the building of Europe

Over and above simply Keynesian management of the economy, most states, in an attempt to correct inequalities, pursued a policy of partially redistributing income. Governments intervened more and more directly in the social sphere by setting minimum wages and working conditions (working hours, paid leave, etc.), by developing education systems and pension schemes or creating social welfare systems aimed at ensuring a minimum degree of security for all. An economy of solidarity developed. Thus the scope of the welfare state increased, according to the philosophy of basing "social security" on the principle of national solidarity:[1] the nation was required collectively to ensure the welfare of all. The least well-off were the chief beneficiaries, even if this measure corrected the inequalities only very partially and patchily.

The shift to consumption

In the context of the 1960s, the prosperity equation was reduced by Helmut Schmidt to its most simple arithmetic form: wages + consumption = full employment. The belief

---

1. No longer on the traditional concept of the employment and insurance contract, which protected certain sections of the population against a limited number of risks.

in long-term exponential growth was firmly shared. Numerous indicators confirmed this curious equation: people in the west become part of a consumer world summed up by just a few words: television, car, sport for all. The image of woman as mother and housewife gradually faded as more and more women joined the workforce from the mid-1960s onwards. This development — an economic necessity and a factor for independence — led to a redefinition of the couple and effects on the birth rate, as well as to discussion on a new apportionment of income and responsibilities. The patterns of consumption of families in western Europe were turned upside down by the combined effects of the huge increase in average purchasing power and the major technological advances paving the way for series production at relatively low cost.

Everywhere leisure tended to become more democratic. This change affected all sectors of the population, helping to undermine traditional patterns of differentiation between social groups and thus the diagnosis in respect of social homogeneity. The notion of social environment was changing. Training and sociability gained increased importance, displacing social boundaries. Poverty took on a different meaning. Was this a revolution in social relations? The trend was towards individualisation, even if the debate focused on the idea of the end of the proletariat.

Maintaining steady expansion

The reduced percentage of manual workers was accompanied, in the area of political and trade union attitudes, by an increase in the options for reform. The industrial model of the 1960s implied the subordination of the human being to economic concerns. This model led to the search, sometimes involving conflict, for an industrial society which would preserve the stability of an expanding economy: such was the task entrusted to politics. The traditional elites, linked to large-scale ownership of land, only partially managed to maintain their position, and in relatively small areas. The links between the worlds of business and of specialists and experts grew closer. Proclaiming that growth and social progress are synonymous, straddling public and private sectors, interlocking with both the political world and the world of culture, the technocracy emerged as the ruling class.

Changing values

Over and above their individual characteristics, people in the west managed to combine productivity and a better standard of living, welfare state and individualism. During the latter half of the 20th century, the increasing similarity between the lifestyles and social and cultural practices of the peoples of Europe could be seen as the fundamental element in the development of a transnational identity in Europe. The universe, now explored, had shrunk; technology triumphed over distance. All the world's capitals were less than one day apart; and through the ether, even less. Even though the spectre of genocide still haunts everyone, a planetary perception was starting to emerge, complementing the cold war in the polarisation of western thinking.

Television, for Europeans now the chief source of information and recreation, perpetuated the dichotomy between two types of cultural consumption, one "élitist", the other entertainment. Beyond this there were attempts to achieve renewal and create a counter-culture, often the prerogative of the young, as a reaction to the entrenchment of a consumerist culture which did not preclude spasmodic rejection. The apparent standardisation of lifestyle and social practices (despite the continued existence of great inequalities) could not disguise the crises born of the rapid and uncontrolled upheaval in living conditions. The 1960s dissolved into disenchantment and disillusionment.

Fracture

Keynesianism, which assumed that the social consensus and price movements were immune to major upsets, was to be short-lived. Social conflicts arose between 1968 and 1973 and upset this equilibrium. At the end of the decade, the continuing expansion of production led to an increase in wage claims, consumer demand, a rise in interest rates as well as speculation in raw materials. Wage rises were all the greater in countries with a weak social consensus. The increasing openness of economies precluded the automatic passing on of production costs to the customer, leading companies to incur debt and reduce profits and investment.

The limits of trade union renewal

The general trend was to appease social conflict. The trade unions, their legitimacy recognised, exerted growing influence both politically and through collective wage bargaining.[1] However, the brutal re-awakening of tensions in 1968-70 showed the limits of this modernisation. Many young workers did not share the concern of their elders as regards employment: Europe is short of manpower. However, with inflation starting to eat into purchasing power, the discontent of heads of families combined with that of the young, denouncing the illusion of monetarism and the Taylorian system, whose rigidity impeded occupational mobility as well as everyday life. The social machinery patiently assembled in the countries of Europe, and particularly in the north, seemed incapable of satisfying these immediate demands.

---

1. The spread of co-management in Germany, or the 'New Society' programme put forward in France by J. Chaban-Delmas after the presidential election in 1969, illustrate this tripartite management.

20

1968: the expression of a paradoxical generation

The spring 1968 crisis stemmed everywhere from the same questioning of the values and operational methods characteristic of western countries. For adult education experts, the chief focus of this crisis was the student revolt. This is probably one of the blind spots of their approach, for the phenomenon was not only a student problem. It was a problem of young people as a whole.

The "rebellion", with those who had been the first to benefit from growth becoming its main critics, is only incomprehensible if one forgets the denunciation of progress and authority — of the family, institutions, the churches, schools and the state. The young were "insolent", the strikes "wildcat". Yet the "confusion" and the "lost generation" were real enough: in the questioning of the model provided by growth, the post-war world order, its economic and ideological bases, the alienation produced by the "one-dimensional" society. The rejection of things was less fundamental than the rejection of values, of forms of organisation, including liberal democracy and the parliamentary system.

The student protest against inadequate resources, the mandarin-like behaviour of teaching staff and the obsolete methods of passing on knowledge, was the characteristic university form of a more general criticism of a consumer society and of its instruments of cultural domination. The questioning of the social and political order was directed at the institutions of state, as the principal obstacles to any structural move towards greater social justice. Which explains why the example of the students spread to the workers, in particular young workers, who were often of rural origin, without any trade-union affiliation or industrial tradition.

The year 1968 left deep scars, helping to change social and cultural attitudes and practices; the major issues of the following decade were first put to the test here: militant feminism, the challenge of the "greens" and "alternative" movements. After 1968, provincial society had yielded to cosmopolitan modernity. And 1968 really did mark the transition from a community-based social structure to a network-based social structure on to which individualism was later to be grafted. One of its chief goals was the community-based structure, but it was no longer to be found. "Unrest" was indicative of a new and complex relationship between individual and group, institutions and state. But 1968 operated in a roundabout way. By asserting that "everything is political", 1968 raised the fundamental question of the areas in which its intrusion was unlawful, in other words the acceptance of diversity of interests, opinions, the way people are, the ability to live without ultimate certainties, in other words all that goes to make up the democratic ethic.

The development of the permanent education ideal was to be one response to these questions issuing from the depths of people's being and from day-to-day living. A response far removed from that of the most determined protesters, and closer to the reform plans for France drawn up by Jacques Chaban-Delmas and Jacques Delors, which aimed to put an end to the omnipotence of the "tentacular and inefficient" state, to archaic and conservative social structures, and to promote social dialogue, to reinforce equality of opportunity, while at the same time respecting diversity and individuality; to humanise relations between government and governed, and to improve the quality of life.

II. The project

Those — be they citizens or educators — who find themselves confronted by this wave of protest and challenged by the questions raised, are fired by a shared conviction. In their work, they have lived through the years of reconstruction. Professionally, they understand the complaints directed at the universities. Admissible though the criticism may be, the consequences which the students seem to draw from it are less so. The industrial revolution lies at the root of a general advance, of unprecedented economic progress. It transformed the material conditions of life, bringing about a qualitative improvement in them through the growing potential for well-being and culture that it released. Technological progress was bound to usher in the age of plenty. This inevitable consequence implies that the essential pillars of growth are not questioned. Prosperity calls for more balanced development instead of the "rapid and sometimes erratic growth we have experienced". According to one formulation, and a decidedly ambiguous one at that, conveys most accurately the positions of the various experts and heralds some of the future developments in their approach: "The necessity for a strongly organised society is more and more keenly felt, as is the necessity for a type of political and vocational guide capable of proposing common objectives and community action (the systems approach) in the field of community development." (2/5)[1]

The experts are anxious to take stock of the situation: Europe had shifted its very bases. The main features of modern civilisation are industrialisation, urbanisation, development of the tertiary sector, mass communication, etc. Nine major characteristics were enumerated in the early reports: a mass, post-industrial society, "feeling its way forward", ("evolving towards functionality"), an informed society, a consumer society, a sub-cultural, organised (planned), functional and frustrated society. In this society, where all the major problems are now stated in terms of mass, they pinpoint the feeling of frustration caused by the uninterrupted chain of never-satisfied needs and aspirations forged by the consumer civilisation; indeed, their satisfaction does not bring progress anyway.

---

1. The first figure refers to the number of the work cited in the bibliography, the second figure is the page number in that particular work.

"The development of communications has placed each individual at the centre of the entire world, but in a cold, abstract way: one knows, one sees, one hears, but one is neither seen nor heard in return. The decision-making centres, like the centres of information, seem to become more and more remote. The reinforcement of bureaucratic traits pollutes social relations as a whole." (3/6) Everything points to the breakdown of traditional structures, reflects the image of individuals who have lost their way, of a social fabric which has lost its certainties, and has no yardsticks for action. To compensate for this absence, the individual joins groups of his own size: intermediate communities of defence, discussion or action; in so doing he merely shifts the problem, for this proliferation of communities fails to have any impact on public affairs. Failing the re-establishment of continuity — no longer merely a question of isolated cases but of people in the mass — between the life of the individual and the "tightly-knit" network of the rights and duties of communities, the inevitable result will be the proliferation of small spontaneous communities, taking refuge in artificial paradises or drifting — always menacingly — towards various forms of absolutism.

The individual's needs are linked to this need to rediscover continuity, to find security in working life, to realise his full potential, to participate in a collective endeavour. "It is one of man's deep-seated needs to be recognised as a partner in and member of a community, and in that community to express himself, to exchange ideas, to reject or accept, in other words, to live as part of a community." (3/6) For the champions of permanent education, man is always a social and political animal.

Industrial society is not democratic enough. If there is to be equality of opportunity, it must exist for all. If democracy writes cheques, the economy must honour them by seeking ways and means to optimise its efficiency. Full employment calls for the best employment. Things therefore have to be corrected in order to be improved. The political democracy that conferred equality of rights therefore evolves, by its own logic, towards social democracy. Participation in action and in the sharing of the spoils assumes a hitherto undreamt-of dimension. Essentially, this task of modernisation must fall to education, through the virtuous circle it establishes with participation. The constant exaltation of participation — the means of transcending all conflict — only becomes meaningful in relation to this faith in education, which itself only becomes meaningful through the principle of participation underlying it.

For the first time, the analogy with industrial investment takes on concrete meaning in education. But an investment without an organisation able to take it and put it to good account remains a dead letter. Society must therefore modify its structures and reorganise itself. The analysis therefore dissolves into a set of virtuous circles: technical progress requires and permits the development of industrial democracy;[1] participation will be its declared aim and means; education must be the principal route for achieving it, at one and the same time the means and the field of application, but also of experimentation.

A new conception of man

The principal focus of the concerns of the permanent education theorists, for whom man is an animal *of* and *in* progress, is the individual, resolutely posited on the basis of two characteristics: every individual is perfectible; every individual is different from his neighbour. These two elements lie at the heart of the primacy accorded to the situations with which life confronts him and which will be challenges as much as learning opportunities. It is therefore not a question of placing him in a straitjacket. Every

---

1. In other words, democracy conceived on the operational model of industry.

individual is engaged in a "natural" quest to improve himself. "This need is inextinguishable and is present throughout life (whether in the personal, social or work field), even though it is not a permanently active motive. ... Until the end of human life, the new directions which will be followed by motivation of the progressive type are limitless and impossible to predict. The classical model of three stages of life (school, work, retirement) is therefore changing at the same time as the educational principles on which it is based." (2/12)

Technocratic ambitions

The world is changing rapidly, too rapidly perhaps, but there is no stopping it. So men will have to be changed, helped to adapt. And in order to do so, the certainties inherited from the past and now obsolete will have to be replaced by new, equally reassuring references. This is the only way of guaranteeing the durability and development of prosperity, progress and democracy.

Man is the chief obstacle to the smooth functioning of social relations because education does not prepare him for co-operation. Lack of understanding of what is required by the new social relations based on co-operation prevents the system from functioning. People must therefore be made to understand what this society is and what these social relations are. The more educated citizens are, the more harmonious will be the life of the community, everyone understanding the necessity for collective discipline. In this way, it will be possible to bring about a new organisational structure, developed by all, meeting the general interest and the product of a conciliatory dialogue between all the forces in the nation. Permanent education will thus be the principal institutional arena of preparation for the society of the future. Here it acquires a triple dimension with respect to co-operation, taking it as its essential goal. Permanent education is the means of achieving it by putting it to the test in everyday school life; and it is the only means of theorising it as end and means.

Modernising social relations means modifying roles and status, promoting change, mobility, transcending ideologies. Choice is what singles out the individual in a democratic world; but this choice must be an informed one: the interplay of viewpoints is merely an expression of the inadequacies of analysis. Ideologies are pernicious. Everything therefore rests on one's grasp of reality, in other words on a positive view of the facts.

Confidence in education, based on the dual idea that everything can be learned and that everyone is capable of learning everything, will develop along two lines:

– if everything can be learned by everyone, it is because there is no discontinuity in reality: according to the technocratic reference of the pioneers of permanent education, the object is gradually apprehended, in stages, each of these being reality; there is thus no room for ideological confrontation. Different viewpoints only attain legitimacy through the stages by which they are gradually explored: hence the idea, pregnant with many developments and ambiguities, of a basic education which is the same for all;

– while everything is a learning opportunity, society must still organise itself so that these various learning processes become possible: this is how a democratic society worthy of the name becomes an educative society.

The notion of educative needs

The progress of science and technology has brought in its train a considerable growth in the "sum" of knowledge, which is renewed at a much faster rate. Aware of this multidimensionality and of the accelerated obsolescence of knowledge, all authors stress the problems associated with burdening curricula still further with the social imperatives weighing upon the education system, *viz*:

- the indefinite increase in the number of persons not working, whether engaged in initial training or retraining, is unacceptable;

- jobs have to be kept and society cannot pay for no matter whom to prepare for any occupation or diploma whatever;

- the job market will fluctuate more and more; people will have to anticipate the need to retrain at some time or other, and so this adaptability to change must be developed.

The gap between knowledge available and knowledge taught is widening. If what is taught today is obsolete tomorrow, it is important to distinguish what is essential from what can be renewed. The idea starts to emerge that, while knowledge is cumulative, education is selective. The solution to this contradiction will be a twofold one:

- first, it reduces knowledge to the conditions in which it is acquired and used: knowledge concerns the individual, it belongs to him more than being an objectivised, fixed product; it is the individual who gives knowledge its relevance and, moreover, it is this which forms the basis of its permanence and integrity. Consequently subjects and centres of interest are expanding. But, although it is born of experience and practice, knowledge must, to become knowledge, be re-articulated in its entirety. It will be the role of representation in adult education to develop this aspect both theoretically and practically;

- once these principles have been established, the problem shifts from knowledge itself towards procedures and methods. So the status of knowledge evolves: dogma of all kinds must be shunned, and an experimental, pluralist, functional and democratic attitude developed instead.

An indictment of school

The advocates of permanent education were to reiterate and systematise the criticisms levelled at the "traditional school systems" in the 1960s. True, an "education system always finds itself overtaken, overwhelmed, by the movement of ideas and patterns of behaviour which reflect the very life of societies." (3/10) But what is the purpose of school today? Should its sole objective be to select and reproduce an elite? School is too egocentric.

It has become more democratic, taking in an increasing number of young people at secondary and higher level. Yet this renewal has not been accompanied by the desired changes. "Educational systems have adapted (even radically so in some cases), but much more through their size and by broadening their content than by changes in their structures and by abandoning their traditional content ... more by addition than by substitution — which partly explains the intolerable decline in their productivity." (2/21)

This is not at all a technical criticism, despite seeking to pass it off as one. It is inspired by a political will. Not only has school failed to reduce social inequalities, but the system actually serves yesterday's elites and not the elites of today or tomorrow. This is an expression of a social position and expresses a specific demand — that of a social stratum realising that education does not secure it access to the social positions which ought by rights to belong to it if "there is to be progress". It is in this light that the fundamental issue centred on culture and its methods of production, distribution and acquisition should be understood.

Adult education is as much engaged in combating the preconception that "culture acquired through 'general education' is more complete and valid than culture acquired in preparing for and exercising an occupation" (2/15) as it is in combating encyclopedism, "a mystification (...) claiming to equip man with a corpus of knowledge sufficient to last him all his life." (2/15) It is therefore just as much attached to its own description, namely that of its values, while criticising a *modus operandi* dominated by the encouragement of passivity, the failure to take account of aptitudes and learning through failure: "This system is opposed to the exploitation of aptitudes, tastes and motives and imparts distortions paving the way for social crises. Anyone who is inadequately or poorly directed helps to upset the functioning of the social order. His misfortune is that of a poorly organised society." (2/39)

From one symposium to another

In 1967, a symposium held at Marly-le-Roi (France) took the concept of adult education a stage further through its innovative aspects, such as the importance of the notion of the needs of adults as the basis of all adult education policy; the integration of occupational, cultural, community and personal aspects and the need for an approach leading to the gradual development of a dynamic, flexible system able to serve as the framework for a coherent policy.

In 1970, with the fifteen reports commissioned by the Secretariat, a consensus was reached: the proposals converged, but few of them were implemented. This last point was to become one of the major preoccupations of the coming years, the basis of a "development plan" aimed at assessing pilot permanent education experiments conducted in the member countries.

As used here, the term "permanent education" does not denote a species of *ex nihilo* creation of the Council of Europe. The term already existed in certain systems of legislation, and forms the basis of a whole corpus of educational practices in various countries. In 1971, the development plan entitled "Foundations of an integrated education policy", adopted by the Council for Cultural Co-operation (CDCC) as its official policy document, sought to "transform this abstract concept, characterised by a long-term perspective, into a more practical working hypothesis, namely the study and assessment of ongoing experiments in member countries." (3/0) Ideas started to crystallise. Permanent education was defined as a comprehensive project, emphasising the need for continuity of approach through all the stages of its development, i.e. during pre-school, school and post-school life. The idea of pilot experiments occupies a central place in this approach: "exchanging experience and becoming aware of common principles will constitute a decisive factor of progress." (3/2)

The aim of the experts[1] is therefore to gather together what exists in piecemeal form, to draw the threads together as fully and vigorously as possible; hence the importance of the evolutionary nature of this approach, whose originality lies in the fact that it does not settle for setting out a series of principles but seeks to measure them against practical reality. It is even more original in that it will sum up these observations in a model it claims is archetypal. Very soon, the give-and-take between theory and practice in elaborating the concept was to give rise to verification of the "progress" of the action taken, measured against this concept viewed as a "yardstick". The various elements stemming from individual experiments are subsumed into the whole — the potential of permanent education. The experiments would be meas-

---

1. In March 1972, the CCC set up a Permanent Education Steering Group of experts from the member states, with responsibility for assessing the pilot experiments. From 1972 to 1979, this group was headed by Mr Bertrand Schwartz, Director in Nancy of the CUCES-ACUCES-INFA Group and a consultant of the French Ministry of Education. His strong personality, intellectual and institutional creativity and tireless energy set their indelible stamp on the group's activity and beyond.

ured against the degree of realisation of the concept, and hence the degree of integration into a developing adult education structure.

Some of the various stages in this process were embodied in projects, undertaken successively or in parallel. In Strasbourg, in December 1977 and April 1978, two seminars on the topic of education for disadvantaged groups focused on the needs of the unemployed, women and ethnic minorities.

From 29 May to 1 June 1979, a symposium was held at Siena (Italy) with the evocative title "Towards a permanent education policy for today". Disenchantment was the order of the day. The hopes of the 1970s had not been fulfilled: "The group found a situation of 'rampant crisis': one is confronted by the lack of any real collective awareness of the phenomenon. Even the most visible and spectacular aspects of this crisis, massive youth unemployment and delinquency, have failed to induce anything but stopgap or repressive measures." (10/18-19)

The consensus that emerged from this symposium related more to the need for a different kind of education than to accepting the model of permanent education. Education was now one way of responding to the crisis. This was clearly apparent even from the topics dealt with by the three working groups (employment and permanent education; territory and permanent education; school and permanent education), which led to a real "Siena Programme", and were in essence reiterated by the Conference[1] marking the end of the "Development of adult education" project.

---

1. Adult Education — 10 years of change; trends for the 1980s. Strasbourg, November 1980.

The system of systems

I. The concept

The strength of permanent education as a project lies not in the structural, institutional or pedagogical changes which it is going to develop and organise into a system. It lies first and foremost in the "anti-Copernican" revolution it proposes, namely, focusing educational measures on the individual. Hence, the first question educators have to deal with is that of the skills people need to be given if they are to live, work and develop in the new type of societies to which we apply the generic term "post-industrial". Man is producer, consumer and citizen. Permanent education, unlike specialised measures, insists that these roles are not disconnected. It is by linking them together in a new way that man will be able to adapt to the social reorganisation which is occurring between work, study and leisure.

The individual will have to be guided towards this future, helped towards an understanding of these changes, shown how to control their development. This guidance relates to individual skills as well as collective ones. It is on the basis of the individual in his actual situation that permanent education is going to draw up its plan. This situation, which varies from individual to individual, will call for various educational responses; the mediation of needs occupies a central role in such action.

Reconciling individual needs and social needs

The needs of adults develop on various different levels — emotional, marital and family, leisure, cultural and even sexual. Let us concentrate on three major categories of needs which are, in turn, expressed as demands on the educational system:

- the need for growth; to produce more and produce it faster; to consume more and sooner;

- the need for cohesion and also for the apportionment of a number of roles corresponding to an internal system of commonly accepted values and rules;

- the need for regulation.

One of the original features of this approach is that it conditions the full realisation of the adult's personality in the concomitant exercise of creation and responsibility. "The desire to control change and to develop scope for independence and personal thinking in all aspects of community, cultural and economic life" (6/24) is particularly strong today. The individual is not only alienated, as certain educators suggest, because he cannot give free rein to his faculties for exchange, play and creativity. He is alienated above all because he is thwarted from "active, participatory life", cut off from responsibility. "Participating in a collective endeavour implies a continuous network of affiliations and solidarities, each cell presenting itself simultaneously as a centre of creation and decision-making for the individual and as a link with increasingly large units. It is because these links do not exist or have become ossified that society is considered as uninhabitable by larger and larger numbers of young people." (3/6-7)

The confines of legitimacy

The fundamental justification for all educational systems is the future, not the past. Its horizon is the free citizen in a "working democracy". Promoting democracy is the basis of all progressive policies in education. But this may take two forms: on the one hand, giving individuals the opportunity to compensate, as adults, for the inequalities of access to the various different levels and forms of existing school systems; on the other hand, promoting a new type of culture production by taking account, in the implementation of the educational process, of the real problems of individuals in their everyday lives. Creativity is therefore as much a consequence as it is a cause of democratisation. In order genuinely to be able to make personal choices, everyone must be able to understand the nature of their aims and the possibilities open to their particular aptitudes. They cannot do this alone: even if "the democratisation of education is founded on self-education, assisted as and when necessary." (7/17) Help and guidance will enable them to make the most of their potential.

Since there are so many cracks in society, it is in the integrity of the individual that permanence must be sought. His willingness, mastery and understanding of the facts must contain the makings of possible development, in other words, reforming the coherence of his system of understanding and analysing situations.[1] "No fund of skills must be neglected. If it wishes to mobilise all aptitudes, society must recognise the right of every human being to realise his aspirations without discrimination." (2/43) Equality of opportunity thus becomes an aim which transcends the simple political idea of giving everyone maximum opportunities. What this will mean in concrete terms is the opportunity for all, without consideration as to age or sex, to mobilise the means ensuring maximum realisation of their intellectual, physical and emotional potential in the area chosen by each individual personally. (7/17) Not obtaining the adult's consent would be unthinkable here.

It would run counter to the principle of the autonomy of free citizens, who must voluntarily come together in order to develop the common weal and democracy. This does not mean universal access to the longest and most theoretical courses of study. "The purpose of the democratisation of education is to give everyone an equal opportunity to structure their thinking."

---

1. Information is an exemplary field, in which what counts is learning to select, from the mass of signals received, the ones worth retaining so that they can be mobilised on demand.

The concept of man seen essentially as a "product" of his society yields to the concept of man as the "producer" of his society, setting himself three main policy objectives:

- to enable everyone to cope with the fluctuating job situation;
- to train "adaptable polymaths" rather than specialists;
- to remove all distinction between general culture and technical or vocational education;
- not to allow anyone to enter employment without vocational training;
- to enable everyone to perceive his place and role in society;
- to de-alienate culture.

Problems of definition

At the Siena Symposium, J-J Scheffknecht observed that "for some, the notion of permanent education has already simply become synonymous with general training", and stressed "the need to clarify the concepts used." (10/17) The definitions of adult education would merely be variations on the different plans developed, the product of this intellectual analysis being organised in the form of a project. From the outset there is hierarchisation. "Permanent education provides this [unified and agreed] concept, while recurrent education appears to be the strategy permitting its realisation." (6/1) The legitimisation of this distinction and hierarchisation is based on the historical character of education and the notion of permanence.

Historically, education is not a transcendent entity, but a creation of society. By and large, its history is influenced by its context. Its nature, content and organisation vary according to needs.

The first aspect of "permanence" is the one it organises in the life of the individual, enabling him to maintain cohesion and coherence between the conceptual structures he uses and the wide range of situations he has to cope with — if not control — during his existence. Another aspect is bound up with the democratic perspective. "Permanent education proposes not so much to raise the cultural level of the masses to the ideological values of the dominant social groups, but to bring the changes taking place under the control of society as a whole, to conduct research on the life systems and underlying values of the processes of change, so that all society can become aware of its own destiny." (2/48)

These elements make it possible to clarify other concepts. *Recurrent education* is fundamentally characterised by discontinuity. It is defined as "a flexible system of alternation between working life and study." (3/50) *Further training* helps man to develop throughout life, complementing and — using the appropriate educational channels — capitalising on the initial thrust of school or university, enabling him to alter his living conditions by himself, notably in the vocational field, so that workers can adapt to changes in technology and working conditions, thereby promoting their social advancement.

Permanent education is distinguished from the above in that it not only assumes the existence of action specific to adults, but also a particular effort as regards the contents and methods of learners. It covers all perspectives according to a process which develops throughout life. Implying a coherent, integrated education system embracing both initial and subsequent training, its aim is to introduce continuity into the process of personal development, so that it is not abandoned to more or less sporadic education. For the episodic return to formal learning, regardless of the reasons for it, is only fully effective if such periods are part and parcel of a social practice which is educational in itself. "There is nothing to be gained from returning to education or training unless work and everyday social activity are accompanied by sufficient intellectual activity to produce the motivation to acquire knowledge which is helpful to personal development and usable in day-to-day practice: permanent education is rooted in a permanently educative environment. This is why integrated permanent education, the sum of the enriched vocational, social and cultural practices offering a background to episodic educative periods, formal and informal, organises both the continuity and discontinuity of our personal development, of our social participation and our schooling." (10/18) There are therefore three aspects to the notion of permanent education: a pedagogical approach, an education policy and a socio-educative aim.

Yet from 1977 onwards, the term adult education made a comeback and achieved dominance, under the pen of Henri Janne, consigning permanent education to the status of "philosophy". From this moment onwards, permanent education was a set of principles forming a "common foundation", on the basis of which the "two levels of the education system (youth and adulthood) must be considered." (7/3)

II. Fields and strategy of permanent education

The aim here is to design a system and assemble within it all other existing systems. The issue is contemporary man, of tomorrow's democracy, at last reconciled to his history and to the progress of science and technology, to the demands of an economy working for his welfare. The issue, rooted in the ideal of the Enlightenment, is also a society of dialogue rather than of ideologies, a society of co-operation, of partnerships rather than of conflicts.

From pre-school to post-school: levels independent of age

There are powerful arguments in support of a complete, integrated education system. This means that there must be an education system which guarantees everyone a response to all their needs on the basis of what they are as individuals (readiness and potential) and of what they intend to do. "Its purpose is to:

- create good understanding between persons with different interests, aptitudes and social origins;
- use all available manpower effectively;
- satisfy the new needs of the labour market and cope with the increasingly rapid restructuring of industry;
- promote better use of buildings, staff and equipment;
- reduce differences in status between the various courses of study." (2/27)

This permanent education will not be something for adults alone. Adult education is merely the testing ground for new teaching methods and new rights. "The sectorisation of school must be reduced; the sharp divisions between primary, secondary and higher education, between general education and technical education, the premature proliferation of branches of study should be replaced by a true, general, basic community education, followed by specialised education or training, as late as possible, and designed from the standpoint of adult further training." (10/22)

Situated downstream of initial education, adult education cannot be wholly separate from it. As Daniel Hameline explains: "the future demand for adult education will never be a rational expression of objective needs, but always at the same time a fantasised expression of desires nourished by the experiences of childhood. It is essential, therefore, for these experiences to be integrative and not regressive,

39

either because education has the air of a happy parenthesis to be reopened, a sign of the irresponsibility of childhood, or because it is feared as a humiliating backward step. In either case, imagery has supplanted reason: dependence and counter-dependence create an alliance of opposites in order to shackle the use of reason." (13/65)

Hence, as regards its decisive role in shaping personality, three major objectives are assigned to the pre-school level:[1] controlling aggressive impulses; learning group behaviour and expanding the environment beyond the home. Considering its role in reproducing social inequalities, positive discrimination should be exercised to the benefit of the more disadvantaged families, and, in this connection, since "the family bears primary responsibility for the development of the child", "the school for parents" and the educational role of social workers acting in conjunction with the family and all other educational operatives within a particular geographical area should also be developed.

This permanent education must be organised so that it can respond to the demands of old age. "The average prolongation of life, the maintenance of health and the social need for the performance of tertiary tasks (requiring little physical effort) make it absurd to cease all work at the age of 60 or 65, which does not mean that working life in the strict sense of the term has to continue." (2/28-29)

The fundamental principle of permanent education will thus be the unity of an educational process embracing the education of the young as well as of adults, seeking to attain coherent goals through coherent means. The

---

1. "At this level, the focus should ideally be socialisation and not instruction. Socialisation must not be limited to family life (reduction in potential roles). It must be a community effort, in which external bodies are also involved (information and research)." (2/28-29)

co-ordination of all the educational establishments and coherent educational content, in other words continuity of the educational opportunities provided, must also be a feature of it.

Between culture and social action

"The illusion that initial training can bear sole responsibility for preparing people for productive life must be abandoned once and for all; initial training and further training must share this function between them: initial training will cater for the aims of independence and socialisation, and general orientation towards active, productive life. Special, occasional training courses will cover entry into productive life and access to the first job, while adult education will cover the continuous adjustment to employment and to social activity." (10/8)

Yet the specific feature of permanent education is that it is not limited to a novel combination of the various different "levels" of the educational process. The early reports reflect the idea that the democratisation of education is incomplete so long as it remains at the secondary level: since the higher level alone leads to careers, advantageous social positions and privileges, these privileges must be broken down by throwing higher education wide open to the masses.

However, the mistake of opening up the system without altering it must not be repeated. If the purpose of an educational reform can be to alter what exists in order to improve it, innovation and alternatives to what exists will be required. The point is to proceed little by little. Integration into a coherent system which is not simply a juxtaposition of existing practices can only be gradual. The world of adult education is a diverse one; its structures vary from country to country, subject as they are to the fluctuations of political regimes, ideological orientations and national legislations. Its very practices differ even within individual countries, at the whim of currents of opinion.

"Such processes entail an immutable succession of degrees or stages:

- determination and development of the need for change (identification of educational needs);
- definition of operational objectives; (analysis of objectives);
- choice of strategy (combination of media);
- implementation of changes; (organisation and assimilation of content);
- assessment and re-examination of the need for further changes; guidance.

It is essential that the planned change should be treated as a complex whole, all stages of which are considered simultaneously and continuously and which must, at all times, engage the active interest of the person concerned." (2/8)

However, this is only an apparent solution to the question, for it actually rests on several different levels:

- the first of these is the integration of the "levels" of education into one global system and, more generally, the integration of teaching into other aspects of human life;
- the second relates to the possibility of conflict between individual advancement and social constraints: how to reconcile the full development of individual aptitudes and the need to integrate individuals into a society whose frameworks impose constraints and where everyone has to take account of other people;
- the third and last relates to whether or not it is possible to alter the education system radically without altering

socio-political structures and, consequently, the need to envisage permanent education systems on the basis of the type of society they will have to fit into.

In 1970, there was a need to overcome the divergences and differences in situations. There was a clash of ideas over the links between vocational training and adult education, between initial schooling and "continued training", between further training, complementarity, personal development, cultural development, "creating awareness", etc. The idea of permanent education is an attempt to organise all these features into a coherent whole. Co-ordination becomes a priority with a view to providing a better response to the needs of adults, giving them reliable information and avoiding duplication, providing a genuine opportunity for the new technologies to serve education on a proper value-for-money basis.

Permanent education is not merely a means of making adult education more coherent. What it claims to provide is a global solution. It is on and around this basis that any national education scheme must be (re-)built. This is a decision for the state, which appears to be the best possible guarantor of the citizens' liberties and equality. Compulsory schooling is thus shifted to the responsibility of states, as a right that has to be guaranteed to every citizen, immigrants included. To some extent, the adult education experiments were only carried out on the initiative of "voluntary" organisations because the state did not meet its own obligation. It is essential that adult education should be placed back in the hands of the state.

III. Transforming education systems

In view of the diversity of national situations and the legitimacy of very open pluralism in the approach to solutions, the potential for change inherent in each system must be respected. Hence there is a virtually limitless range of possible versions as a result of national, historical and cultural circumstances, of systems, income levels, social pressures and so on.

One favourable factor that deserves to be noted is that the demand for education can only grow under the combined effect of democratisation, the general prolongation of compulsory education and the need for vocational retraining. "As a backlash from the mass media, growing sections of the population are becoming aware of the gulf that separates them from a standard of living or culture that has become a consumer goal. Latent needs are emerging in the individual and collective consciousness, merely by virtue of the fact that knowledge of how others live is now much more quickly acquired and in far greater detail." (3/10)

The following are some of the unfavourable factors:

- "the lack of adequate education and information, enabling citizens to understand the place and function of the education system within the organisation of society;
- the problematical nature of fundamental political action, owing to lack of commitment and pressure for change;
- the fact that school systems primarily serve the needs of a social minority whose attitude is conservative;
- the existence of sectoral behaviour among teachers and administrators, which prevent them from fully playing their role as agents for change;
- the inadequate involvement of representatives from the world of work and the administration and local authorities in developing the education system;
- the inherent sluggishness of an over-centralised educational bureaucracy." (10/19)

"As long as the educational establishment has the air of a protected sector with its own special lifestyle, facilities and conventions, as long as teachers continue to adopt an attitude inherited from and maintained by a tradition protected by isolation, there can be no hope of major changes." (2/46)

Insufficient practicality

The picture here is necessarily patchy. "In pedagogical terms, our project might perhaps result in overall proposals which could form the basis of matching experiments in the various countries; in institutional and financial terms on the other hand, it will have to be limited to conceptual proposals, whose usefulness and operational character will vary from country to country, and will be of much more relative and much less practical value." (7/23)

In most countries, education systems were very profoundly affected. The unit-credit system, continuous assessment, allowance for experience, practical participatory teaching, open universities and schools are some of the innovations which took institutional shape. Side-by-side with these, alternating education schemes and extended use of training leave were developed. A type of education covering all working life developed in a growing number of member countries. A number of them attempted to define a coherent system by incorporating a right to worker training in their legislation. The educational system also opened its doors to adults under various names — adult education, popular education, social advancement, recurrent education, etc. But it is above all the last-mentioned form that became established under the influence of various types of paid training leave. As often in such cases, the political will had to adapt to and find expression in systems whose tried and tested coherence had resisted innovation. There was no integration in a vast global system under an integrated concept. Similarly, it cannot be said that, throughout life, every individual has the possibility and the opportunity to go on learning.

For the Council, this lack of success could not fail to affect the state and progress of the debate. Indeed, this debate was to undergo a shift under the twofold influence of the resistance of the existing educational coherences and of the consequences of the economic, social and cultural crisis. The idea of permanent education thus shifted substantially, all authors being aware that there were conflicts which were bound to snowball in the future, such as:

- conflict between the aspirations of individuals and the demands of society;

- conflicts of interest between social groups which benefit from the existing systems and those who consider they foot the bill;

- ideological conflicts in the models which define the ideal type of society, of which the education system would thus be the driving force as well as a reflection;

- "structural" conflict between all established systems and their potential replacements: changes, even inevitable ones, are feared;

- conflict between all societies and their educational systems.

The title chosen for the final conference was an eloquent one: "Adult education in the context of permanent education". The conclusions were sometimes almost bitter: "Today [school] serves almost as much to exclude as to promote; this can be seen, for example, in the number of young people leaving school without any vocational qualifications, thus at best feeding the secondary job market." (10/20)

The main transformation was applied to pedagogical methods in adult education, where it had already taken place! However, the studies carried out showed the unde-

46

niable importance of gathering together in one coherent whole what before was merely tentative and do-it-yourself. The second positive factor was to "label" these initiatives and to bring their various promoters within a single concept. There is no doubt that, here too, incalculable progress was made in increasing the practicality of methods, techniques and legislations. Most practical was progress in the field of vocational training programmes for adults, and then, with the crisis and its dramatic repercussions on unemployment, in the various programmes set up for those sections of the population particularly affected.

Polarisation of the "vocational" and the "cultural"

With the economic crisis, the areas for intervention by the educational organisations found themselves facing new demands. A recentering of the instruments, tools and skills they had developed over the years then became clearly apparent. A clear polarisation could be observed, grafted on to two different readings of the crisis. Two divergent strategies set out to find an answer to it: the goal of vocational integration for individual purposes on the one hand, as against the cultural goal with a collective aim on the other.

The contribution by Gaston Glaesener (Walferdange Centre, Luxembourg) provides the best illustration of the first of these two aims. Focusing on the relations between training and employment, it is concerned with the difficulties encountered by young people in integrating into working life. The overall shortage of jobs combines with the unfavourable trend in the demographic structure and the mismatch between the profiles of young people and the jobs available. The responses will be linked to finding and getting a job; side-by-side with measures aimed at making a certain number of jobs available to young people, steps are taken to facilitate the transition of the young person into working life: introductory courses and career guidance courses organised with a view to familiarising young people, in practical terms, with the demands, prospects and satisfactions of working life.

The UNLA project (Italy) illustrates the second aim. In the education project for providing technical assistance to biodynamic agriculture in Campania, Anna Lorenzetto presents the mobilisation of "all local forces with a view to promoting, in a poor area remote from any opportunity for industrial development, a series of socio-economic and cultural initiatives born of the area itself and capable of giving a new lease of life to the people in this area." (9/32)

The divergence between these two approaches only increased during the years of crisis. It seems that, owing to its very principles, the Council of Europe could not help but show greater interest in the latter; it is this which perhaps indicates another area of growth, another area for development. "In other words, this is a project for creating a new kind of day-to-day living; a project for the quality of life." (9/30) Taking this approach a stage further was to be the aim of Council of Europe Project No. 9.

Second stage
CDCC Project No. 9 —
adult education and
community development (1981-86):
counteracting the crisis at local level

The pain of crisis

Traumas and hopes

The Siena Symposium of 1979, mainly attended by decision-makers from the various countries, was still divided on the scope and nature of social change: the educational strategy adopted differed depending on whether the crisis was a transient one engendered by the accumulation of economic and social problems in the national economies or a change in the world economic order — in other words *ad hoc* management or structural measures. At the Council of Europe, labour market analysts and economists helped to bring a new approach to the problems of adult education. There were two decisive contributions: by Henri Janne on flexibility and by Professor Saverio Avveduto, entitled "6 000 days ahead of us", a tribute to the last text written by the Italian futurologist Aurelio Peccei. Employment prospects are almost exclusively a matter for educators, who by virtue of their geographical location are part and parcel of the local fabric and are beset by the increasing demands of individuals already in the process of losing their jobs or afraid of doing so. As the months pass in a crisis which is everywhere growing more apparent, recognising its structural character is going to become imperative.

A thorough redesign of the European socio-economic environment

Europe's importance in terms of world population, in the production of goods, in the emergence of new technologies and new values, had been constantly shrinking. The central event in this process was the dynamism of the "yellow countries" which, it was feared, could spell the inexorable decline of Europe, and not only the loss of influence of its economic and social organisation on the world stage.

The long period of recession reduced the capacity to create jobs and led to rising unemployment in all western countries. In 1983, there were some 33 million unemployed in the OECD countries (as against 10,1 in 1970). From 1973 to 1981, the abandonment of farming continued in the EEC countries, involving some 2 million individuals, while industry registered 5 million redundancies, linked in particular to the continued spectacular reduction in employment levels in manufacturing industry. The proportion of service workers in the EEC rose from 50,5 % of the total to 56,5 % in 1981. People questioned the industrial paradox that "industrial decline" goes hand-in-hand with the spread of "industrial methodology" into every sector of the economy. The first "workerless factory" projects were a further source of anxiety.

The impact of the new technologies, from microelectronics to computers, from telecommunications to new materials and biotechnology, was impressive. Yet this snowballing permeation of the production apparatus and fabric did not have the anticipated effects, which led people to question the equation technological development = employment growth. The new technologies brought economics in the three classical factors of production: energy, equipment and above all — a very sensitive issue — labour. The resulting unease stemmed from the impossibility of deciding between the fear that technological development "does not necessarily mean new jobs, but perhaps precisely the opposite" and the hope that the positive effects would ultimately prove to be merely delayed, in the long term impacting on employment with the emergence of new products or modes of production.

According to the fashionable development hypothesis, based on the theory of long cycles, while technological

52

innovations might lead to another growth phase within a long cycle, this would not be before the nineties. The immediate future therefore seemed destined to be one of sharply reduced employment. Further, analysts stressed another equally worrying phenomenon: the polarisation of qualifications, in other words, "dequalification caused by the growing automation of tasks, with its obverse of over-qualification, called for by new tasks and the emergence of new occupations". The picture of the future for observers in the early 1980s was thus of an increase in low-skilled jobs and fewer jobs at the top, in other words a lowering effect overall. Also, over-qualification threatens the better-educated: of course they will have the advantage of the best job opportunities, but at levels that do not correspond to their training.

The growing scarcity of jobs focused the attention of the public at large on immigrants, the young and women in particular. There were strong differences of opinion about how to cope with the crisis where immigrants were concerned, more or less serious, ongoing attempts to improve literacy and incentives alternating with repatriation incentives. The main problem posed by the young was the transition to employment and how to manage it. However, the feminisation of jobs focused attention more: this difference was probably attributable to the revolution in habits it represented; it was certainly not as spectacular as proclaimed by feminist circles, albeit profound and radical all the same. This feminisation represented the paradoxical fruits of progress. But women were also to be the chief victims of the reduction in jobs and the rapid growth in atypical jobs. This situation was certainly crucial to the emergence of the idea of community development.

Recently, there has been evidence of a certain recognition of local characteristics, with various forms of regionalism as the symptomatic and controversial expression of this trend, which only serves to encourage the development of complex social policies. Characteristically, therefore,

Europe is seeking to integrate what have come to be called sensitive sections of the public and disadvantaged areas, at the same time claiming to promote diversity in patterns of thinking and models for organising people and geographical areas.

I. The questioning of reference models

Attitudes are marked by uncertainties: "In only thirty years we have moved from the great myth of economic expansion to crisis, from questioning general (but unevenly spread) welfare to cutbacks and the ethics of retrenchment, from infatuation with science to a religious revival and, from the standpoint of our particular concerns here, from the aim of carefully planned social development to the resigned but conscious acceptance of what each day brings." (14) There is one certainty that cannot be avoided: the traditional recipes are no longer appropriate. There has to be a transition from a defensive attitude of combating unemployment to a more positive approach of fostering employment.

The fall in the growth rates compels a reconsideration of the entire economic strategy. Instead of strategies to promote strong growth, which create industrial jobs but entail subordination to economic forces and, consequently, social exclusion and the deterioration of everyday life, what is needed is a more balanced economic and social development policy, less subordinate solely to the laws of economics, and restoring quality of life and work to their former places.

Emergence of the local

The crisis does not affect all sections of the population in the same way: new investment and job creation are occurring in advanced technology sectors and providing work for the most highly skilled. The areas most affected by the crisis are both those "left behind by growth" (rural areas)

54

and regions of traditional industry, those which were historically the first to undergo the industrial revolution, and whose decline has gathered momentum since the end of the "golden sixties". A host of measures have been taken to cope with this, such as redeployment. Desperate though the race between creating and destroying jobs may be, the widely varying size of economic units offers distinct opportunities for development: unlike regions of mono-industry characterised by marked structural rigidity, those whose economies are structured in the form of small and medium-sized units seem able to take advantage of quite substantial flexibility and alternative possibilities.

Another consequence is that the spread of new technologies into all areas of life is leading to territorial re-organisation. Electronics, new materials, energy, communications and so forth, all these technologies call for a new distribution of space, a different assessment of the combined effect of production factors. "The importance attached today to non-material investment shows the importance of an economic approach based on local measures turning human resources to account. Further, micro-activity is no longer of secondary importance [...] Small establishments are now "hooked up" to national and international markets." (22/7) The emergence of new centres of development and the decline of former centres of industry confirm the marked disparity in the situation from one geographical area to another.

Much of what was taken for granted during the period of growth are now called into question. The crisis is as much a cultural as an economic one. The hopes of yesteryear have soured into disillusionment. The value of change is stood on its head. For Professor Walter James, consultant to Project No. 9, change continues to play a dissociating role. What was novel yesterday becomes commonplace today and will be outmoded tomorrow, be it material goods or ideas. Progress no longer has the character of inevitability previously ascribed to it; man's future depends on his capacity to accept that choice is possible. Technologies transform work for all into unemployment for many. The traditional social forms by which the members of society express their independence have regressed. The family is tending to shrink, more often to become a single-parent family. The attraction of towns and cities, the opening up of hitherto isolated regions to the modern world and other migratory factors make the homogeneous community a rare species, threatened with extinction.

The spectacular and particularly painful side of short-term unemployment should not blind us to the lack of long-term prospects, the decline in self-confidence and confidence in the community and involvement in community life, and the accompanying profound changes in social structures and lifestyles. Hence, under the pressure of economic imperatives, most European countries question the way public services are organised and run. Above all, there used to be a belief in the efficiency of the — more and more professional and often institutionalised — public services provided for the public in an increasingly bureaucratic form. On the principle that economic growth would cover the cost, new services were constantly created, adding to the multitude already in existence. Slow growth requires a choice of priorities. Many governments contemplate, if not the actual dismantling of the system, at least radical reform, while the overall economic situation leads to the rapid impoverishment of some people and hence to greater need, precisely when the traditional means of participation created in the post-war period are reduced or eliminated altogether.

II. A new role for education

A number of scenarios for political intervention emerge which, after the initial ambiguities, will lead to different practices, particularly in education.

The first option for intervention is industrial restructuring: the supply side has to adapt. The essential feature in this process is going to be a marked trend towards flexibility; "less clear-cut identification of tasks, rather than emphasis on functions". A large range of unskilled, low-paid jobs, largely done by women and young people, is going to be deployed. For educators, the role of human capital in the development of the employment structure clearly depends on training. Even if the theory of job polarisation cannot be overlooked, the main point is the skills and flexibility of the labour force. The new jobs will require a higher level of training and technical knowledge than the jobs eliminated did.

A second option arises out of a reaction against this sectoral point of view and is concerned with promoting local development. In the process it diverts the concept. "The concept of local development was first advocated by alternative movements wishing to substitute local decision-making and socio-economic organisation for centralised development based on government decisions and the strategies of industrial groups. The traumas of the drift from the land or the first waves of the industrial crisis subsequently led the centralised states or the European Community to pursue a policy of 'revitalising depressed areas'. The point here was, through external over-investment, to enable a particular geographical area to create a new kind of development capable of resolving *in situ* the dysfunctions identified (population exodus, desertification, impoverishment of the economic fabric)." (22/3)

This second option claims to be more comprehensive, considering local development as a factor of social innovation as much as of productivity and based, to that end, on the notion of activity. The educators then forge the specific notion of development training. "The creation of development training policies is undertaken more from the standpoint of integrating sections of the public in a living entity than from that of a social assistance policy. This aim leads to the improvement of the overall productivity of the economic system by improving the efficiency of administration, the employability of marginal sections of the public, the exploitation of local resources, the development of individual and collective initiative, learning to live in society, learning to participate, and receptivity to the outside world." (22/5)

The education system must be restructured in relation to these future demands. The ideas put forward for the promotion of permanent education remain valid ones, all the more so as they do not neglect the "local" element. Saverio Avveduto sums up the basic question as follows: "What is the dynamic and what is the limit of adaptability to national vocational training systems and industrial redeployment measures, at a stage when technological development and industrial redeployment are accelerating? Ultimately, what is the "sensitivity" limit of human resources? There is no doubt that there are limits to the adaptability of human resources to economic development, regardless of the policy adopted, and these limits are regrettably confirmed the greater the duration of the period of unemployment, depending on the age of the person concerned." (13)

In view of the mismatch between school education and the needs referred to, permanent education and retraining seem more flexible and capable of rapid reaction in the short term. Adult educators find this interface with local development interesting. Even if the preceding activity broadly confirmed their approach, providing it with the essential theoretical frameworks and giving it institutional legitimacy, particularly at Siena and Strasbourg, the fact nevertheless remains that the essential edifice, permanent education, the underlying concept that was to serve as a matrix for the systematic organisation of the systems, has misfired. On the contrary, adult education seemed, in the early 1980s, to be eclipsed by vocational training measures. In the absence of existing practice, adult education was seeking a theoretical framework to supplement the framework conferred upon it — in its internal function at least — by the concepts of permanent education and which theoretically organised its social place. The field of local development seemed to provide this opportunity, one immediately grasped, leading to the reorganisation of the concepts of the combinative adult education programme.

The aims of Project No. 9

Siena: the "turning point"

Essentially, the argument runs as follows: the resources at the disposal of the centralising state tend to eliminate the specificity of local communities[1] and to unify them. The development of mass communications has merely added to the phenomenon and created a culture of "the masses", which urbanises even the rural population and brings individuals into an isolated pattern of consumption (juxtaposed but without true relations). However, the cultural questioning process, awareness of the dangers of "conditioning" and homogenisation represented by this dominant culture produces defensive reactions: either withdrawal into "privatisation" or an effort to restore or create local communities.

CDCC Project No. 9, "Adult Education and Community Development", set out to determine the contribution of adult education as a factor of economic, social and cultural innovation in local and regional development.

The project consisted of a joint study of 14 pilot experiments selected from the 70 proposed by governments. The aim, through detailed co-operation between those conducting the experiments, was to enable them to improve their practice by taking into account the successes and setbacks of those concerned and to use these

---

1. "In order to become a sociological reality, a human community must establish a network of social relations between its members and be experienced by them. These relations must be specific to it, even if the members of the community, as is the case with modern societies, find they are involved in relations of all kinds with individuals and groups external to that community. But a community may also see its internal relations dwindle and gradually lose all substance to the benefit of external relations integrating its population within a broader social unit (generally society as a whole)." (11/12)

experiments as the basis for developing instruments of use in new situations.

Three sub-groups, termed "co-operative development groups", were set up on topics common to certain projects. On the basis of the provisional results of 1984, the Project Group defined two principal guidelines for summarising, disseminating and utilising the results with a view to creating a multiplier effect. These were to open up the co-operation process to other experiments; and to develop national or regional networks (or improve those already in existence) with a view to establishing transversal links making it possible to co-ordinate the work of innovative experiments in integrated local and/or regional development in the member countries.

Three meetings were organised during the autumn of 1984:

- community development responses to unemployment which take account of economic perspectives;

- development of roles of women for participation in community decisions — decision-making structures;

- prospects of co-operative monitoring.

Lastly, eight joint seminars were organised in 1985 in co-operation with the authorities of the member states, on topics proposed by them, to test how far the proposed measures for action and experimentation could be applied in different social, cultural and economic contexts.

I. The notion of community development for adult education

Project No. 9 was based on a twofold hypothesis: "Community development is based on the conviction that the population must become a producer and an agent for development in the community and that it can learn to become this." (18/6) The whole question is to ascertain how this participation can and must be organised in order to become more efficient. "Collective actions" are the most immediate guide for any such approach. From its inception, permanent education assigned the following tasks to adult education:

- to start out from the specific problems of people;
- to help to solve problems;
- to take account of all the conditions for solving problems (whether individual, collective, educational, social, economic or political);
- to tackle these problems as close as possible to where they arise;
- to create situations in which adults assume direct responsibility for their own training;
- to develop the critical function of training. (5/33)

However, community development remained marginal to the central aim of providing an educational response for individuals or groups: more than a mere parameter, but certainly not an operational goal.

Yet a number of factors were to play an important role in the creation of a theoretical reference corpus. To begin with, the local and collective bodies were confirmed as the authorities taking the initiative in education. In this way, the local level becomes the focus of demand and needs and the organisational basis of training. The use of the notion of proximity was to blur the distinction here between its geographical and conceptual connotations. A further step is taken on the basis of the notion of "descolarisation" linked to collective actions.[1] Lastly, and above

---

1. J-J Scheffknecht supposed, for the organisation of such actions, that:

- training would become a collective function and would be integrated into the problems of the development of the community;

continued on page 64

all perhaps, training is considered as a social commitment and the trainer as the agent of change. Whether consciously or not, all trainers convey a political message; they can be either agents for maintaining the status quo or agents of social change. "The role played during the training process by the immediate social context (educational institution) and the indirect one (social integration framework) is decisive. Hence all trainers must be prepared to take this dimension into account in very practical terms in their immediate practice." (5/9)

II. Education for development

Where the community is concerned, the notion of development undergoes a change of meaning. It no longer describes the trend of employment and wealth quantified by the growth rate, but "a type of development with a territorial basis through the exploitation of all the natural, cultural and human resources." (22/12) The aim is to grasp all the opportunities that arise, to support new social dynamics: more balanced, more human growth, turning its back on the imbalances which are regarded as the cause of the recession. "The new economic order will need rural areas which have regained all their vitality ... For its part, urban and above all peri-urban concentration, although responsible for housing and an environment which has caused most of the "social fallout" we are familiar with, will increase between now and the end of the century and will call for all the more interventionist an economic and social policy as the social fabric there has been very largely destroyed." (10/30)

- the community would obtain or acquire the financial resources that it could manage;

- trainers would come from the community;

- the community, responsible for its own training policy, must be able to call on a specific function, that of the "development agents", in order to assist it in its task.

64

Education for development is first and foremost teaching responsibility and the will to change, encouraging and supporting the galvanisation of interpersonal relationships and community exchanges. A certain tradition of adult education finds that it too is altered. The idea had been to change the environment; now it will be to develop it. The concept of man as "maker of society" now gives way to that of him as maker of his environment. "The development of the roles of men and women is not fundamentally a solution that can be pursued solely on the basis of individual development as conceived by the liberal, humanist tradition characteristic of the uniform weave of the rich and varied tapestry that is adult education in Europe. Also, fostering in individuals a critical awareness of their condition ultimately implies the wholesale questioning of the social, cultural and economic structure overall. Furthermore, the action which follows this type of idea implies the mobilisation of collective rather than individual responses." (18/80).

Educating man to create his own environment

I. Developing social creativity

Concepts of community development

Permanent education developed on the basis of a new conception of man and society. The breakdown of the consensus weakened traditional solidarities. The project group devoted its efforts to rethinking the educational dimension of community development, not without a certain amount of conflict between ethics and economics. For Walter James, adolescence has become the permanent state of the human condition, "ceaselessly reinterpreting reality. There are no longer just a few simple role models (...) Life in all its aspects is less and less a matter of certainties to be demonstrated and more and more a question of hypotheses to be tested. The music of our lives is less and less composed for us by others: we now improvise like jazz musicians, listening in our relations to hear where others are and creating harmonies with them." (26)

For other writers, what counts is to focus adult education on the issues thrown up by the economic crisis and its effects on the social fabric. To find alternatives, greater demands have to be placed on the potentialities available. The ability to manage one's own existence must from now on be envisaged from the standpoint of the social, economic and cultural factors which condition it. Far from being challenged by the territorialisation of adult education, the necessity for every adult to be trained throughout his existence acquires a new legitimacy.

The remodelling process must also give concrete form to the types of link between two hitherto antithetical domains: culture and social action.

In the first place, culture is expressed individually and collectively by the desire and ability to ensure that people achieve fulfilment, either as individuals or as participants aware of a community. Strong condemnation is reserved for the sort of education that seeks to share among the greatest possible number the achievements of a fossilised culture, "already acquired, summed up in cultural products, in riches locked up in books, museums, the knowledge of experts [which needs] to be passed on to all individuals or groups, treating them as singular, isolated entities: some communicate, the others consume." (13/163)

The search for alternative, pluralist models implies that the sub-cultures are allowed to develop. But this does not mean that the marginal groups have to be imprisoned in a ghetto, depriving them of the culture of the dominant class. Jettisoning the "democratisation of culture" — which either rejects sub-cultures or "legalises" them to the point of elimination — "cultural democracy" aims to link the sub-cultures to the "universal" cultures by making them aware of their own values and those of others. Viewed thus, "cultural democracy denotes a process during which culture escapes from the culture-education pairing, shifting it towards the education-politics pairing and making it the context for action involving the whole community. The experiments conducted to this end make people "aware", and are not afraid of this leading them to question the powers that be." (13/163)

Another line of demarcation was to be drawn, this time with respect to social action. The notion of educational assistance occupies centre stage. Educators are very familiar with these forms of action targeted at priority groups; they also know that these forms do not reject their marginality. On the contrary, they accept it as the inevitable consequence of a socio-economic system in which the technical division of labour leads to social divisions; in which it is the function performed that determines each individual's value. The adjective "priority" merely indicates the fact of "preceding". This assistance to marginal sections of the population fulfils a conservation function. It is now not so much a question of remedying the phenomenon of marginality as of regulating or even eradicating it as a problem.[1] The aim of the new political education will be to consider marginalisation as the act of "taking up a position on the fault line of society and equipping oneself with the means for remedying it. It therefore takes a stand against the social division of labour; it therefore attacks the problems of wages, housing and health.

Education for community development also tends to distinguish itself from the excessively short-term imperatives of qualification for the system of production. There is no doubt that arguments in favour of a territorial approach to permanent education are determined by the state of the economy. If it is at the local level that the most dramatic effects of readjustment occur, it is at this level that new economic revitalisation strategies will become meaningful, depending on the degree of integration of the various elements. Whether rural, industrial, mountain or urban areas, they are subject to recession and have different priorities.

Any decentralisation of initiative depends on the scope for mobilising populations. The urbanisation which took place during the period of growth was based on the industrial type, paying scant regard to the quality of personal development and social life. Yet this does not mean that localising initiative is a guarantee of a more democratic system. However, the Project Group was particularly careful not to fall prey to naive "grass rootsism", attributing every virtue

---

1. The pitfall here is the action organised on the pattern of medical care: diagnosis representing the definition of the public's needs; the disease and its remedy representing the contexts for and types of intervention; the medical staff representing the creation of a network of educators. This model is reassuring in that it suggests that all can be "cared for", reintegrated into the social fabric. But it supposes that the ills and needs of the individual are defined at the sites where they occur. But who can claim to do this in educational and cultural matters, without reducing the quality and specificity of certain social structures?

to local and community life and worshipping at the altar of the new myth that "small is beautiful". The micro-regional context is the place where knowledge and action mutually enrich one another by their proximity. More active and better informed social participation is the pre-requisite of more egalitarian local development, and a guarantee of the sort of local development which may succeed in curbing the abuses of central power.

However, the micro-regional context continues to be inad-equate "to the extent that the correctives to social and regional inequalities are initiated at the national or inter-national level and that, more generally, the central power continues to be the site of the decision-making or co-ordination required by major orientations and major national, regional and local equilibria. Nothing could be more unacceptable than to encourage people to 'manage' their own dependency and inequality. There is also the danger of excessive individuality whenever local action is not confronted by government demands and constraints. Lastly, the increasing ascendancy of the multinationals in all areas of national activity calls for action backed up by national and supranational organisations. But the concen-tration of economic power must be accompanied by the deconcentration of educational power." (10/30)

Two characteristics emerge from this analysis: the pre-eminence of the community and the comprehensive nature of the action. Without in any way excluding the possibility of outside inputs — especially since equilibria and priorities which transcend the local or regional per-spective must be respected — the development will be endogenous: the operation must remain under the con-trol of the local community; the national and international levels whose responsibility this is must support the projects and give them time to mature. Also, action which con-cerns only part of the population, "neglecting and even attacking another part", cannot be classed as develop-ment. All the individual projects (job creation, activities, cultural measures) together form one overall project for the region, the locality and the community within it. All development projects will be based on a specific problem, a crisis affecting the inhabitants, unemployment, an ageing industrial fabric, under-development, out-migration. To this should be added the absence of a community identity and, in certain cases, the destruction of cultural and social values, the consequences of over-hasty industrialisation and urbanisation. Clearly, raising awareness is not only a first step in a development project. It must continue throughout the project's existence.

Autonomy of the educational

The central notions of permanent education are thus reintroduced into the new dimension of the community. However, the focal issue is the autonomy of the educational in relation to the techniques of development. In dealing with this issue, adult educators are going to base themselves on a diversity of means but also on linking these together in order to lock development into a positive, global dynamic. Admittedly, educational action will seem to be just one potential instrument of action for development, but at the same time, and above all, it will seem like the whole of that action. As awareness-raising and the promotion of a group by itself, community development merges with educational action: "Collective development offers each member of the group the chance to take charge of the action of all. ...But this development runs the risk of eluding all regulation in so far as it is comprehensive, in other words, takes into account all problems indiscriminately, and in so far as no one attaches any meaning to it. The community only bestows meaning upon itself by serving as the medium of collective development action, if not a process of cultural democracy, in which the project can no longer be distinguished from the action, in which the action can no longer be separated from the creation, by a group, of its own identity." (13/ 174)

The need for change and the desire for development

The starting point of any educational process lies in the desire to transform what is "undergone" into control of the situation. But one of the first difficulties is to overcome resistance: for although change is desirable, this does not mean that it is desired. It is frequently accompanied by fears, by uncertainties which have to be removed if one is to proceed to the development stage. In other words, change is not synonymous with development, even if it is recognised as an indispensable condition of it.[1] In order to create a development project, this — objective as well as subjective — need for change will therefore have to be spelt out, and the resistance associated with fear or ignorance overcome.

Moreover, the naive belief that resolve alone is sufficient is a temptation to be resisted. What specifically characterises innovation is the always more or less conflictual relationship with the surrounding system. This "conflict" is an indispensable part of the management of any development project. Change always precedes development. Yet the specific nature of education in a community development scheme will not be established by these distinctions alone. What counts is to show that education is not a fortuitous factor in action for development, so fortuitous that one could just as well dispense with it. There are two parts to the argument:

– first, showing that development is not a particular technique administered by specialists, but on the contrary is inseparable from the community where it takes place. It has already been established that the latter was a

---

1. The pioneers of permanent education had already stressed that "training should not take place unless those concerned have jointly taken a political decision." (2/8)

phenomenon of the will not an almost mechanical consequence of the development of the social and economic context. Even more, it has to be shown that
development is merely the apparent dimension of the
work of the community acting on itself. It is the community becoming aware of itself and changing. Hence,
to speak of the "technique" of development would be
tantamount to usurping, confiscating one of the powers
of the community itself.[1] Education and development
will thus be synonymous, the issue being ultimately
political;

– second, learning to become an agent for development.
The process of community development is based on the
conviction that the population must and can become
an agent for the development of its community and
produce that development. Above all, the development
process supposes that growth, and then the crisis, have
above all engendered a certain passivity among individuals and groups. In order to become an agent for
development, one must therefore first learn how. "The
promoters of projects [believe] in the necessity of preparing the individual to become the agent of his own
development; for helping him to abandon the role of
spectator in favour of that of actor, to "act" instead of
"react", and lastly, to consider himself not as the object
but the protagonist of action." (18/46)

---

1. "The notion of local development covers a great many strategies, a
great many practices. The formalised, definitive definition of the notion
of local development is hard to implement. [...] Local development must
therefore be considered more as a "practice", as a way of managing a
local system. Studying these practices makes it possible to identify a
number of characteristics which, "for a given time and space", may serve
as a provisional definition. [...] Local development reduced to a "recipe",
to a "product" would soon be obsolete, whereas development as a
method of management makes it possible to integrate the various data
related to its implementation as and when they arise. What today forms
part of a development policy will be integrated into everyday life and will
appear as simply one pillar of local life". (22/2-3)

The repoliticisation of civil society

Development projects are inseparable from the region, the locality from which they stem and derive their meaning. Education is the solution of continuity between change and development. Contrary to a technocratic decision, development involves people's wills, harnesses them in a common project around which the promoters — and not just the initiators — are going to meet. In pluralist and democratic systems, this will is never easy to create, nor is it completely homogeneous. It is the result of a complex process involving various social agencies, with different and divergent interests and ideologies. The fate of a problematic region will ultimately be the result of a consensus, the concrete expression of the many power relationships which will have come about.

Consensus

A certain conception of political life and of its battles linked to private interests helps the promoters of permanent education to distinguish its aim from those interests, somewhat in the manner of a referee standing back from the scrum. Here one encounters a certain conception of civil society contrasted with the conflictual nature of politics. Behind this idea, there is of course autonomy of development requiring a consensus. Educators are particularly sensitive to the fact that, in most cases, unanimity must yield to a relative consensus. The education project will always emphasise what unites rather than what divides and serve the interests of the community rather than private interests. To the question who is able to judge this common interest, the educators reply that only permanent consultation between the various components of local life will produce the minimum consensus necessary to the pursuit of integrated educational measures.

Thus, education is not merely one of the means of development; it is its very method. Awareness of the machinery makes for better control of it and can lead to more active and better informed social participation, the condition of more egalitarian local development. Hence one decisive consequence: if the aim is still to develop active, creative attitudes and if one can see a reaffirmation of the principle that knowledge and action mutually enrich one another by their proximity, the task of defining the problems of the immediate environment is going to acquire a fundamental dimension (rather than a preliminary one as in the formative process of permanent education) — in as much as it also concerns the way they are dealt with and solved.

Divided views on autonomy at the local level

Community development makes the debate on inequality the very core and starting point of its actions. Yet educators are not even agreed about the possibility of combating these inequalities: this raises the issue of the relationship between educational action and social structures: permanent education had already claimed a political role for education; but, once within the domain of culture, it somehow remained in the lofty world of ideas. With the Siena Symposium, community development brought it back down to earth. Project No. 9 was to sharpen its focus by instancing any number of specific examples of inequalities in the pilot experiments: inequalities in industrial society, in the urban environment, in under-development, in the rural environment, in male and female roles, etc.

At the root of all the projects lies the same basic, explicit belief and confidence in the individual's capacity for change. The individual is presumed to be capable, by learning, of becoming the agent of his own development. A majority of promoters consider that the objective will have been achieved if, at the right time, they provide those concerned with the requisite support and information. However, some of them point out that individuals are the product of a certain determinism in social structures, which is not without effect on their capacity for development. In other words, all potential development requires that there should first be a profound change in certain of society's structures.

If the aim of all the projects is to reduce inequalities between categories in society, the fundamental question then becomes how to choose the processes of change. Two trends emerge:

– on the one hand, those for whom inequalities are bound up with social structures; for them, the measures required must take as their aim the removal of obstacles preventing individuals from achieving true equality, or at least, alleviating its effects;

– others, without denying the existence of such obstacles, advocate a less frontal attack: in other words, such politically radical action would result not only in the alienation of the persons who are the subjects of the action but also in the destabilisation of persons and agencies engaged in development work.[1]

The problem of "raising awareness" emerges again in the need to analyse situations and so make them easier to deal with. Moreover, certain projects are very clearly slanted not to the disadvantaged but, on the contrary, to those who, since they have the ability to set up businesses, may later create jobs. It would thus probably be an over-simplification to seek at all costs to identify a duality since there is a multitude of possible aims, tactics and even methods: there are some who think that the task of

---

1. This seems to have been particularly highlighted as regards inequalities between women and men. "This fundamental dualism is also reflected in the details of the various schemes. On the one hand, some programmes are specially aimed at enabling women, in certain situations, to engage in activities from which they would otherwise have been totally excluded. Other programmes aim to extend women's field of activity and to develop their involvement in traditional or non-traditional activities." (18/53)

raising awareness must focus as much on those who produce various forms of discrimination as on those who are
the victims of it.

Others give priority to certain groups which are discrimi-
nated against. Some people focus on ideas and theories
rather than on actual experience, whereas other pedagogical approaches favour more formal education of the
lecture-discussion type. Moreover, the role of the trainers
themselves is not absent from the discussion, aimed at
elucidating the nature of this mediation which could prove
to be merely transmission or reproduction of the dominant values. All educators apparently recognise the power
of exploring the awareness and perception of reality as
pedagogical processes. "The real distinction is therefore
between those who resorted to these procedures because
they would raise questions they wanted examined, and
those who avoided these methods because they recognised that they would raise questions capable of destroying the solidarity and unanimity of the group (for example, by introducing opinions and commitments of political
parties in situations from which the latter had been ex-
plicitly banished)." (18/53)

So there are unquestionably limits to the autonomy of the
local level, as there are to the individual's opportunity for
development. The emergence of the local level is here an
indication of a redeployment in the linking of determinisms; the capacity of the local level to renew structures
and regulating systems is just one of the hypotheses relating to the future. Any action in this area must endeavour
to deal with the fears and anxiety which characterise the
end of an era by an effort to define and clarify the uncertainties. With the dissipation of certain illusions developed
in the 1970s, when what counted above all was to make
the system more efficient, the economic crisis revived the
debate. Is the goal of development to smooth the rough
edges, to overcome resistance? On the other hand, can

one think of any genuine alternatives? The question was not settled then, nor has it been now.

II. The structuring axes of development training

Participation of the people

"The primary resource of a local community is its human potential, its history, its identity, the social and vocational skills of its members. Mobilising them is the primary factor in all action." (17/31) The participation of the people is at once the basis, the goal and the dynamic of development. It is as much bound up with the quest for legitimacy of action (local development conceived as the local affirmation of decisions) as it is with the effort to make it effective. Local development is made up of continuous interactions between various agencies; wealth of expression is thus synonymous with activity and dynamism.

Planning development

In the context of growth, full employment is the central concept of policy, which combines with the postulated link between education and qualifications in determining the equation between concomitant growth of the need for skilled personnel and educational demand. Various conflicting ideas emerge, summarised by Matteo Alaluf (9/2-3) into two main groups. The "economic" view considers the education system as a "supplier of optimally suited labour", so that school has to be adjusted to foreseeable production needs. The cultural view holds that "school needs" govern economic structures. The education system must train people in accordance with their nature, needs and personal development. Industry must be capable, in all circumstances, of offering jobs which match individuals' skills and their need for self-fulfilment.

However, the contradiction between these two views stems from the same pedagogical illusion: in both cases, the "labour demand" variable (number and types of jobs) is regarded as a given; it is the "supply" variable that training influences. The economic viewpoint is part and parcel of a policy of employment and education, accepting the form in which the labour demand presents itself as a constant and consequently aiming to adapt the labour supply; the cultural view, on the other hand, conceives of adult education only outside the realms of production and vocational training in the form of cultural and community activity.

Against the economic thesis, it must be said that there is no single way of organising labour and no single "optimum" employment structure for any given type of occupation. As for the cultural thesis, it accepts "the school system as it stands and all the attendant social conditioning networks which tend to reproduce inequalities and social determinisms. The extent to which choice of school and occupation, like personal aspirations, are a function of the social and family environment is well known. So it is conceivable that this merely serves to reinforce the whole machinery of pressure and social determinism, in the very name of the unfettered development of the individual."

Community development seems to be a way of transcending these problems because it focuses on micro-planning. The purpose of interaction between the various different planning levels is to avoid not only the "one-way process", in which the plans are transmitted from the top downwards for scrutiny and implementation, but also the spurious "two-way process", which permits no more than largely negative feedback from the bottom to the top, and is supposed to encourage the higher authority to make adjustments in order to reduce the desired level of performance locally. There is another type of feedback, regarded as more constructive, which consists in indicating to the higher authority the practices it should alter and the constraints it should remove to enable local activities to flourish. This is bound to stunt the development of local projects obliged to aim for certainty in the short term: "The local projects which have succeeded are those in which it has proved possible to aim at long-term targets and to implement, in the medium and short term, the measures necessary to attain those distant objectives." (18/42) This results in three types of requirements:

- not to confuse the "experimental approach" with "short-term planning";

- to plan development finance not for a limited period but on a long-term basis, so that projects do not collapse when "special" finance ceases;

- to remove legislative obstacles.

Different educational planning (including education outside the official education system), implies the creation of a network of communication and participation through which all those concerned can effectively participate in the process and also in the management of decision-making. In each case, planning must not be a problem of professionals but a process in which the various "users" have a genuine right to be heard. Not only during the planning phase but also during the implementation phase, it would seem indispensable to give participants ways of constantly adapting the system and curricula to their needs and inspirations, in order to create a permanent process of modifying strategies and new needs, a process based on experience and also on discussion and analysis.

Secondly, the definition of education given means that links and co-ordination are required between educational planning and planning in other fields: education will not be dispensed solely in educational establishments. In turn, this means that sectoral planning conducted in a vacuum and co-ordinated only *a posteriori* is inadequate.

The obligation to co-operate

The new practice considers persons and needs first, and makes the education dispensed a consequence, not a determinant, of the process. The education provided must align itself with this reversal. The principle whereby the type of education is decided *a priori*, and the "benefici-aries" later persuaded to accept it, is erroneous. The objectives of education and training must be defined on the basis, not of formal postulates, but of development aims formulated on the basis of needs for change which have actually been identified and must take into account the material and human resources available in the community. This calls for an awareness of the nature of reality as a whole, which includes social, economic and political elements and calls for a comprehensive approach to problems and for a co-operation strategy geared to this goal.

There are two aspects to this requirement, which is fundamental to any development project: on the one hand, the permanent enlargement of co-operation at the local level to include the greatest possible number of protagonists involved in local life; on the other hand, the essential link between the local, regional, national and international levels in order to utilise all available human and material resources, and to co-ordinate action as efficiently as possible. This duality has several different dimensions.

First, the appropriation of the various components of the local situation at which the action is going to be targeted. It is dealing with problems piecemeal which has led to non-development. The furtherance of local development can only be obtained by an effort to pay greater attention to the overall nature of problems; assembling the protagonists will therefore be indispensable, but must be reinforced by co-ordination to give it meaning, through:

– setting up bodies for consultation, co-ordination, decision-making, application and assessment, all of them without exception including the competent local and regional protagonists for all sectors of the life of the community and independent of them;

- making it the primary objective of these bodies to meet the minimum conditions for as broad a consensus as possible, not only regarding the causes of decline but also, and perhaps above all, regarding the objectives common to the various sectors.

A second aspect is the scope for achieving economies of scale and greater efficiency with no increase in cost. There are various pressures acting in this direction:

- in a period when resources are declining, or increasing more slowly, ruinous competition must be ruled out;
- innovation is so rapid and widespread that only closer contact between the bodies responsible for innovation can permit effective dissemination through the whole system of the innovations produced by a few individuals but useful to all;
- while duplication of the services provided by various bodies is not always a real problem, the fact that the system overlooks specific categories in the services it provides is a serious shortcoming everywhere.

The third and final aspect relates to the development of the monopoly of education. The shaping of knowledge determines both areas and fields of action. The added value of co-operation here will be the cross-fertilisation of systems of knowledge/practices. It will be stimulated by the fact that:

- the objectives set need at least to be understood, and if possible accepted, by those who could be in a position to facilitate or prevent their implementation;
- educational skills exist in the community: those who possess them can be called upon;

– associations are powerful vehicles for ensuring that the community contributes to adult education.

III. Institutional training

The co-ordination of operators does not occur spontaneously. It presupposes that they will learn and change instead of wanting and waiting for others to change while preserving an image of themselves which they regard as immutable truth. Transforming the various organisations of the community is something that can never come entirely from within. In community development, this transformation must enable the community to refashion the organisations for its own development. In this respect it presupposes greater communication, making it possible to identify the strong and weak points of the organisations, as well as a desire to share control with others. "It is probable that, even when legally independent, the educational apparatus will increasingly come under the supervision of a governing body and/or will be heavily influenced by groups whose goal is not education as such but the aims it serves. (...) Increasingly, [the educational bodies] respond to needs defined by other people, and help to provide this response in the context of a broader mandate. Education therefore increasingly places itself at the service of development and, if it maintains or increases its professionalism, this is less and less in its own specific area." (18/43)

Questioning the compartmentalisation of training

The work of training is far too often regarded as the preserve of specific structures organised on the basis of the type of public concerned (i.e. age groups) and of the general goal of (basic and further) training. The internal between the various training structures do not make for optimum use of educational structures. However, the existence of training structures that are "clearly identified" in social life constitutes an ideal means of contact with the population. Decompartmentalisation is therefore one of the goals of productivity, as well as being an opportunity for links with everyday life. A local development project will transform:

- the teaching curriculum, adapting it more closely to everyday life;
- the roles of professionals;
- those responsible for supervising teaching curricula, and also those who devise them, into persons who enable others to contribute in a way they consider to be important;
- the school system, which traditionally separates children from the community and isolates them from all adults, with the exception of the teachers.

Integrated into everyday life and its problems, organised by all, used for the purpose of directly improving our situation, what the Steering Group considers to be an "authentic structure of lifelong education", is above all another conception of training based on the specific problems of a whole community, whose adult members are responsible for defining the objectives and whose educators in large part come from the community itself.

Traditionally, the identity of the educational system has lain in the distance it maintained *vis-à-vis* the other social structures. Its involvement in development compromises this situation through the multiplicity of the interrelationships it promotes between the bodies concerned. Moreover, the pilot experiments provide evidence of a certain advance in this respect: above all, the local and regional networks give rise to an exchange of information or of co-ordination of separate measures; in the course of their implementation, the focus is on collective planning; at this time, learning and development are no longer perceived as a series of activities but as a whole, "a set of educational, social and cultural activities, co-ordinated or integrated, economic or structural, which help to promote local development." (10/32)

Community development brings about substantial development in the monitoring and production of knowledge. "When what counts is learning to promote development, knowledge is acquired and organised by the members of the community themselves, reflecting on their experience and seeking to modify its unsatisfactory aspects. In this context, the problems therefore relate essentially to the production and use of knowledge." (18/4) This knowledge is not intended to promote competition between individuals, nor to help one group dominate another. It is acquired through collective and mutually supportive action, which it seeks to recreate or reinforce; it must bind, not separate. Informal training will play a prime role in this process: it is often a complement to training courses for marginalised groups, because it can provide very practical help in mobilising broad sections of the population to participate in the development project.

The group as an essential factor in the educational process

Here, the group is essential to the learning process. It ensures a supportive atmosphere and structure, in which the adult can acquire the confidence needed to understand his problems. It also enables individuals "to recognise that others suffer from the same constraints as themselves and that they will only get rid of their sense of oppression through more charitable relations between men and women, though there should also be greater social justice between the sexes." (18/75)

Education is too often an activity separate from life. Isolated in a school building, pupils are taught by professionals in various subjects; for the entire period of their studies, they are excused from the day-to-day duties which are precisely what distinguishes everyday life from school.

Community development blurs this distinction, reintroducing everyday concerns into education. "The more education invades the territory of social policy, the more it is designed to promote knowledge of public matters, the more the bodies which encourage it must endeavour to give special treatment to public affairs. ... It was recognised that an understanding of public affairs was a means and not an end in itself. It makes for more informed intervention and a clearer view of possible changes. But productive intervention requires more than information alone: it must be planned with care and executed with skill." (18/76)

The question of access to education

"The very strong awareness that certain persons were not affected by adult education in no way led to the assumption that it was not possible to affect them." (18/69) Once the purpose of training is development, it becomes crucial for those most in need of that development to have access to education; and for no group to be left out. Although it has hitherto generally been considered that the principle of equality of opportunity provided its own justification, this can now no longer suffice. The measures to be taken include the creation of ways and means of assessing needs and offering guidance towards solutions; greater flexibility of action, avoiding imprisoning education in a restricted timetable and geographical framework; the development of special programmes specifically designed to enable the participants to advance at their own speed.

A new principle of polarisation

The contribution of training to development involves a re-ordering of the various functions of the educational. The concepts which form the basis of its organisation are from now on specified on the basis of social integration, social advancement and fitness for employment. Taking marginal target groups into account creates new needs as regards the learning of "social culture". The fact that this type of training corresponds more closely to the spirit of mutual training, in which it is the contribution of the person being taught that is crucial rather than that of the training itself, must also be taken into account. Further training can also help to stimulate the labour market. Lastly, training is starting to be strongly geared to the topic of employability in a context where the technical and economic prospects remain ill-defined. "This difficulty can only be resolved at the local level (at least as regards practical knowledge of the development of technologies, the organisation of labour and manpower management methods)." (22/27)

Third stage
Adult education and social change (1987-93):
rebuilding adult education:
a response to democratic challenges in Europe

The problems

I. Strategic approaches

When Project No. 9 was completed, the crisis was taking a worrying international turn, particularly in Europe. The CDCC reached very broad consensus on the need to make adult education a permanent feature of its programme. (CDCC (86) 42 rev.). It seems that, although the tools, instruments and methods of adult education have been extensively developed, its aims still require clarification. Despite its coherence, and perhaps because of it, lifelong education is above all a framework and in no way the "system of systems" that was imagined. Community development has opened up extremely fertile prospects, but carries within it the twofold risk of the splintering of educational practices (by rejecting what is unrelated to it) as well as their dilution (by its supposed subordination to ideas which are after all external to it).

Added to these elements, which call for a review of the principles of adult education, is the desire to escape from the problems of "change". The notion of social change will be better suited to getting needs and projects into perspective, to specifying them in political terms. As early as 1987, a memorandum providing general guidelines set out the topics the CDCC was dealing with at that time: exclusion, marginalisation, the breakdown of solidarities and social redundancy being its central concerns. Since large-scale measures have failed in combating unemployment, the true nature of social change needs to be considered. The Council of Europe initiated an essentially political questioning process: while not ignoring the problems of adaptation, the discussion tends to focus on the new roles of individuals and groups and their consequences for education.

Where development and those involved in it are concerned, two sections of the population cause particular problems: the long-term unemployed and the elderly. The reasons are different but the result is the same.

The long-term unemployed seem to be both the consequence and the origin of the impossibility of development. Their lack of skills has exposed them to long-term exclusion from the job market. As the result of a "vicious circle", the long-term nature of this exclusion further erodes their skills and increases their vulnerability on the job market.

As a result of policies to combat unemployment, the elderly are excluded from working life. But quite apart from this economic measure, the demographic trends are clear: ageing is inevitable.

A threefold objective is therefore assigned to the new measures:

– on the basis of observation of the educational initiatives taken to meet the needs of the long-term unemployed and the ageing, to inform people:

– on the one hand, about social changes as revealed by the increasing demand for education;

– on the other hand, about the profound changes occurring in adult education in the field, under the influence of a complex demand, stimulated by partnerships made on the basis of local emergencies;

– to define how adult education can enable individuals, groups and communities to cope with the problems confronting them owing to structural changes in society;

– "to highlight the conditions required to make adult education an investment for improved integration in a constantly changing socio-economic environment ...".[1]

The priority is in the urgency of the solutions that need to be found for currently disadvantaged social groups (passive consumers, the socially excluded, the "new poor", etc.). The resulting social problem is a twofold one:

- a constant increase in social costs;

- a considerable loss in terms of human resources (being of no use to the community for years on end).

The employment and economic situation have worsened suddenly. Our yardsticks, our human resources, training and employment policies have all proved totally inadequate to the task of coping with this situation. Emergency solutions have been thought up for maintaining the balance and cohesion of our societies. It is patently clear that most countries have turned to informal education where it was available; where it was not, they have endeavoured to create it, or have turned to the periphery and margins of the formal system.

Through the diversity of the functions it can perform, adult education is very often used as one of the regulatory mechanisms:

- in combating against long-term unemployment:

- to provide training and education which will unlock new employment opportunities;

- to provide general education which can serve as the springboard for more extensive personal development, such as literacy and communication skills, mathematics, introduction to new technology;

- to enable jobless adults to adjust to their situation through constructive management of their time;

---

1. CDCC (87) 28.

- to promote various kinds of personal development, e.g. intellectual, creative, physical;
- to provide support for the ageing:
- to enable them to manage their time constructively and in a manner compatible with their new financial situation;
- to keep up social activity;
- to satisfy the need for culture and relaxation;
- to combat social isolation and passive consumption.

Prior to any rationalisation in the interests of greater efficiency, the practical forms of its mobilisation first had to be observed in order to systematise its characteristics as alternative forms of education. In this way, new intervention strategies can be found, in particular for public service staff, but also for those working in adult education, as well as new tools and new ways of using the tools which already exist.

The project can therefore be expected to stimulate the interest shown in adult education and to broaden the frame of experience of those involved in it. Also, since contacts at the international level are rare, a further aim adopted is for the transfer of ideas and strategies. Yet the brief is explicit: the final product will be less a common educational tool or a new set of rules than a permanent debate on the aims and methods of adult education and the manner in which its problems are formulated.

II. Realignments

The decisive acceleration of history

The temporal context of this project has been an era witnessing the decisive acceleration of history.

Western Europe

Western Europe is dominated by the dynamic process of strengthening the European Community, which is taking it to the threshold of the Single Market, and hesitating before embarking upon Economic and Monetary Europe.

The 1980s are first and foremost the years of deepening crisis. There are several million job-seekers, most of them confused young people, and the disadvantaged, not forgetting those "excluded" from the headlong modernisation of industry. Like their children, these people are under-educated and under-skilled. They are the first to be affected, and for the longest time, by changes in production, the new job requirements and the different skills required. They suffer from the crippling defect of "under-employability". Their major difficulties are not those of access to culture, but the gradual decline in their living conditions, emotional poverty, loss of self-esteem and the associated self-confidence, the lack of a future. They are the "non-public of education".

1985-90. The European Community returns to a higher growth rate, reflected in a sustained rise in employment and a significant fall in the numbers out of work. During this period, 9 million new jobs are created. This favourable trend brought about a fall in the unemployment rate, which fell from a maximum of 11% in 1985 to just over 8% at the end of 1990. From that time, a slowdown in economic activity can be observed, with effects very soon on the job market.

A rapid rise in unemployment then sets in. By the end of 1992, 13 million people are jobless. These trends mean that, at the end of the first half of 1993 over half the member countries of the Community have unemployment rates higher than the "record" level attained in 1985. Faced with this worsening situation, the primary concern is therefore to combat the spread of joblessness.

In large measure, the phenomenon of joblessness is structural in nature. The strong growth in employment observed in the Community did not engender a proportional decline in unemployment. Of the 9 million jobs created between 1985 and 1990, only 3 million went to unemployed persons. In Europe, a rise in employment is recorded after a 2% growth in the GDP, while unemployment does not begin to decrease until the growth in GDP reaches 3,5%. The origin of this sluggish reaction of unemployment to economic growth is the increase in the size of the working population. This imbalance between supply and demand in the labour market particularly affects the so-called "high risk" groups in the population: young people, women, elderly workers, unskilled and/or poorly educated people. Lastly, the proportion of long-term joblessness within unemployment also reveals the structural nature of joblessness in Europe. Today, almost half the unemployed have been without a job for at least one year. This structural component must therefore be taken into account in efforts to combat unemployment.

Western societies are currently confronting the challenge of managing the consequences of the crisis. Whole territories and populations are afflicted by economic restructuring. There are not enough jobs to go round. Groups of able and willing workers are brutally expelled from gainful employment, while able and willing youngsters cannot get into the job market. Alongside these growing masses of people who have been excluded — and for some it will be a long-term phenomenon — from the job market, shortages of qualified manpower are also appearing. The economy thus finds itself blocked at both ends, unable to take off due to a lack of manpower capable of meeting its requirements, and unable to provide stable employment to those who rightly consider themselves to be capable of productive work.

Job creation and economic growth are closely linked, even if this link varies depending on place and time: it expands or contracts in relation to trends in labour productivity. In the face of strong competition from countries with low wages and the weak growth of the advanced industrial countries, wage costs constitute one of the principal elements in a country's competitiveness. In Europe, wage costs also encompass the social component of employment. In recent decades, labour productivity gains have been strongly influenced by changes as numerous as they are diverse: the gradual shift of employment from the secondary to the tertiary sector, the boom in part-time work, technological progress, the replacement of labour by capital, competition from low-wage countries, etc. All these changes have necessitated painful adjustments and adaptations in the advanced economies, whether higher unemployment or growing numbers of low-paid jobs. Every country is affected to some extent by these far-reaching changes and there is a great temptation to find national solutions to this phenomenon.

We are now witnessing a trend towards the relocation of economic activities, in the secondary sector especially, but sometimes also in the tertiary sector (computer technology). The driving force behind this relocation is the lower standard of social welfare and/or lower wages in other countries, whether inside the Community or outside. A new international distribution of economic activity is therefore starting to take shape before our eyes, with all the attendant consequences for employment.

For years, full employment meant both a collective (employment for all) and individual (full-time employment throughout one's entire working life) definition of work. Today, it is the collective aspect which has come to the fore, that is to say providing employment for the greatest possible number by job-sharing, since employment is still one of the preconditions of social cohesion in our societies. There are a number of avenues that can be pursued in this area.

Sharing the available jobs, including the newly-created jobs, is an idea which is gaining ground. Part-time work, temporary work, fixed-term contracts, early retirement are all ways of adapting to the flexibility, mobility and adaptability now required of work, as well as ways of organising more flexible "career" paths.

Central and eastern Europe

During these same years, the obsolescence of the model instituted by the October Revolution and frozen in place as a result of the cold war becomes more marked. The apparent stability had disguised the death throes of the system. In Europe on the other side of the "iron curtain", the world crisis had an even more marked effect on people's lives. The ideological cement now ceases to be relevant; like the dictatorship of bureaucracy, authoritarian planning has demonstrated its inefficiency. Despite efforts at the centre to achieve integration, the coherence of the bloc breaks down. In general, what people want is an improvement in living standards and an easing of restrictions. Young people are increasingly opposed to the unchanging conformity of the system; the working class emerges from its lethargy; the technological elite grows impatient, despite the privileges granted them by an ossified bureaucracy. These groups join forces with the dissident "intelligentsia" in calling for more effective participation in decisions.

Those in power, faced with the problems of maintaining their hegemony against the growing strength of these new forces, seek new politico-economic formulas different from the traditionally dominant Leninist model. A varied range of situations can be therefore be observed, the two extremes being Ceaucescu's Romania and Kadar's Hungary.

Against this background new forms of protest develop. Larger and larger sections of the population are susceptible to the attractions of the western democracies. The desire for change is going to find a more permanent expression than before; increasingly shared by society as a whole, they will find a useful organisational basis in the principles of the "3rd basket" at Helsinki.

Apart perhaps from the questioning of the Marxist dogma in connection with the economic problems, it is above all human rights (arbitrary movement of people, discrimination, etc.) and the nationalist factor which form the substance of the demands put forward. The movements associated with 1989 will be those of civil society, finding, as the Polish movement showed, structures for expressing their views and mobilising the impetus for change.

Between spring 1989 and summer 1991, the equilibrium established after the second world war collapsed with a speed which was all the more disconcerting as it had been inconceivable only a few months before and since, contrary to all expectation, it occurred without major revolutionary violence.[1] The desire for democracy won the day over totalitarianism. A system thought to be immutable fell to pieces in the space of a few months. This was the system of the Party-State, the monopoly of the party over civil society and political life, its absolute control over the police machine, arbitrariness enshrined as a principle of control. It was a system characterised by the privileges of the Nomenklatura, the impossibility of free expression and the prohibition of independent modes of organisation.

At the close of this brief period, during which the peoples of central and eastern Europe, even more than at the dawn of the century, will have "shook the world", some people fancied they saw in it the definitive triumph of one economico-political system. Misled by their own inability to understand these phenomena, blinded by their own dogma, they claimed to see in it the "end of history". This

---

1. If Romania was an exception to this, the reason perhaps lay in the special nature of the "formula" developed by the "Conducator".

was to underestimate the diverse nature of peoples, the tenacity of structures, the weight of the legacy of the past, the necessarily slow rate of social reconstruction apparent today. For this unprecedented movement which, outside the former USSR, will have affected 125 million out of 500 million Europeans, has not provided a solution to the enormous debts of the peoples' democracies, to the nonperformance of the production systems, to the inefficiency of the distribution systems, to the paralysis of the "command economies" and so on.

Central and eastern Europe are currently engaged in a general overhaul of their driving mechanisms: this process must accompany the transition towards a competitive market economy but also — and in a more decisive albeit less spectacular manner — a change of mentality, established social patterns, concepts of the world, society, employment, etc., all require fundamental reconsideration. It is essential to identify new reasons for living together, to forge new attitudes, to democratise generally. As in the west, there is a necessity for an education capable of providing vocational and cultural training, yet also covering concepts, attitudes, behaviour, the basic social skills of citizenship within a democratic framework.

Europe as a whole is therefore faced with a twofold challenge: how to maintain and improve its competitive position on the international stage while, at the same time preserving the social dimension and ensuring the economic and social integration of its individual citizens.

Current dramas, such as unemployment, poverty, conflict, retrograde ideologies, economic deadlock — all force educators to re-examine their approach and methods. Once again they are being called upon to take part in the construction of durable, pluralist democracies, and this leads them back to the very source of their legitimacy — the task of nurturing citizenship. The situation in western Europe is essentially identical: we have become aware, both of the emergencies we face, and of the inadequacy of existing responses. Now that countries which, until recently, were spared the collective drama of long-term unemployment are sadly discovering it, now that communities are in confrontation, now that the great equilibria have been overturned, the questions arising from these developments oblige us to forge a new education for adults. The revelation of the 1970s was the affirmation that the individual would have the opportunity to engage in a range of occupations over the course of his working life. The realisation of the 1990s is that everyone will experience this discontinuity not only in his working life, but also as a "social animal", in his identity as a citizen. In consequence, adult education must not simply enable the individual to adapt to changing circumstances: it must take a pro-active stance to equip each adult to cope with these ruptures affecting all his activities and the whole of his being, and enable him to manage the multiple uncertainty arising therefrom.

Today the task of preparing for tomorrow is no longer merely to facilitate the acquisition of essential skills and knowledge. In a time of social change, adult education must play a fundamental role in the construction of democratic structures and the affirmation of human rights in societies where knowledge has taken on a new and crucial role. Here resides its new legitimacy.

III. Comprehensive education for sections of the public in difficulty

Worsening unemployment

In the 1980s, Europe faces the prospect of millions of unmotivated people, whose qualifications have deteriorated, and who are likely to become completely unemployable. All countries are pursuing intensive policies, yet unemployment continues its terrible upward course. Because of the multiplicity and interdependence of its constituent factors, long-term unemployment is a structural reality which resists both analysis and traditional measures for dealing with it. The population affected by long-term unemployment appears extremely heterogeneous in relation to the target groups which receive help in finding a job. Hence the ineffectiveness of the general measures for tackling long-term — and very long-term — unemployment.

The increase in the duration of unemployment and its widening to include new groups confirms the need to break with the policy of providing assistance to the most disadvantaged and instead develop counter-cyclical measures and attempting to counteract the selectivity of the market. Once this line of attack is chosen, various problems arise:

– as regards targeting: Should the measures taken and access to schemes be reserved for persons unemployed for over a year?

– as regards goals: Should the aim be placement in a "normal" job or should new forms of employment integration be developed?

The action taken is twofold: on the one hand, measures aimed at other sections of the public are brought in and adapted to fit the specific characteristics of the target group; on the other hand, novel formulas are developed, taking account of individual handicaps associated with long-standing exclusion from employment.

In fact, the category of long-term unemployment is either too broad or too precise for educators. The long-term nature of unemployment, its most salient characteristic, is compounded by its recurrence, at least as regards persons for whom unemployment is the dominant, but not the only, fact of life for a protracted period. The "quicksands" effect is a third aspect of it: the harder the economic situation is and as the duration of unemployment increases, the chances of finding a job diminish. Contrary to what a superficial impression might suggest, an upturn in employment does not directly benefit the long-term unemployed. It is more a structural mechanism that operates here, related to the selectivity of the labour market and the process of the social production of exclusion. Thus it is these three aspects that must be considered.

Ageing

According to V. Egidi,[1] "only in recent years has it fully dawned on people that demographic ageing in the developed countries, and particularly in Europe, was a veritable revolution, whose consequences affect and would continue to affect the economic and social organisation of our country." Ageing is first and foremost an individual experience: work comes to an end, one kind of income is replaced by another, patterns of consumption change, marital life alters, health declines... These changes do not always result in handicaps, are not always abrupt changes, even if they call for permanent solutions. Some are brutal — the loss of a spouse — others gradual, and less clearly apparent.

Running counter to these individual events, society decides who is old: through age-related measures (the age of retirement for instance) and stereotypes. It is in relation to this second aspect that the question of demographic ageing and its consequences arises, a source of distress and confusion in the industrialised countries. How can one fail to question the profile of a population group whose life expectancy is almost 80 years or even more, while fertility is barely adequate to ensure renewal? There is much talk of the danger that, as they grow older, our societies may turn inward upon themselves and adopt timid, conservative positions, a development which would

---

1. Tendances démographiques actuelles et modes de vie en Europe. Conseil de l'Europe. SEM (90) 4, Strasbourg 1990.

be all the more worrying since the ability to adapt and innovate needs to be demonstrated now as never before. Other people are already forming associations to combat the omnipotence of the "grey-haired". Ageing cannot fail to produce major changes in values and behaviour patterns. Can it be tackled without a serious crisis? Are we moving towards an "Age War"? This situation highlights two requirements: the need to question these phenomena, but also the need to enable everyone to preserve their capacities and means of action for as long as possible. Educators must endeavour to find a response to this.

By and large, the issues confronting educators go beyond the specificities of the main target groups, that is, the long-term unemployed and older people. A superficial analysis of the situation would place these two groups squarely at the centre of things, primarily because of their shared exclusion from employment. In fact, however, this fact arises from other, more fundamental considerations: the very existence of these groups is linked to industrialisation, a form of "safety-net society", and to a democratic form of the Nation-State. In other words, such groups do not exist independently of the regulatory mechanisms of social systems as they have been developing since the 19th century.

The socio-economic dysfunctionings which educators are called upon to remedy cannot be interpreted singly, nor even as specific to given categories. What is needed is a global redefinition of the workings of society, and this cannot be limited to the parameters affecting the economic situation alone.

Ageing is just as much a problem of social reorganisation and redefinition as it is a personal one. And, looking beyond individual case histories of unemployment, the very concept of unemployment is imploding. A range of related phenomena arise in conjunction with long-term exclusion from the workforce: deteriorating work skills, loss of income, eroded self-confidence and an amputation of one's citizenship. These collective phenomena, in which feelings of guilt and uselessness vie for dominance, affect whole sections of the social fabric, impacting on their internal vitality as much as on the relationships between social groups and, ultimately, on the democratic compromise itself.

Education is therefore now opening its doors to hitherto unfamiliar sections of the public, who have unusual demands and for most of whom the answers education provided were usually school-based and unsuitable. To some extent this is a re-run, in different conditions, of the "democratisation" of school that took place in the 1960s and which, as we well know, largely failed to implement the required changes in its working methods. However, in individual terms, this "invasion" of education by adults contributes to the emergence of a new demand for training. Responses determined by local emergencies and new partnerships are starting to develop, giving education a new look.

Five years' activity and some 30 study visits and seminars have prompted a reappraisal of the question of social needs and a certain distancing from the initial problems posed. Clearly, the upheavals Europe has experienced during this period have also necessarily influenced this reorientation. The collapse of the Soviet system has been the most obvious of these. However, this should not cause us to overlook the multi-dimensional changes that European societies are undergoing in the social, economic, institutional and cultural fields. In Europe today the jobless, the illiterate and the poor are numbered in millions.

The concepts, bodies and machinery designed and developed to regulate economic growth and social cohesion gradually seem to be losing their relevance. Full employment, social protection, the regulatory role of the Nation-States and so forth are prime examples of this increasingly redundant machinery.

The principal conclusion which emerges from the studies conducted by the Project Steering Group, and confirmed by the discussions at the Strasbourg Conference in May 1993, relates to the definitively structural nature of the present changes and to the emergence of an "information-based" society, breaking away from the previously dominant industrial model. In no circumstances will short-term measures prove equal to the task of tackling these changes; they call for a renewal of all the production and social regulation machinery, with education in the forefront. Further, the modes of interpretation and the grids for analysing the social dynamic need a thoroughgoing review; in particular, those which tended to see nothing but the crisis, blinkered as they are by the arena of economics and technology.

Social change

I. Breaking with the dominant industrial model, managing information

The development of data processing technologies in all their forms is the most important event of the closing years of the century.

The third dimension of matter

In 1942-43: Bell Corporation engineers bring to light an observable physical unit, whose use improves the transmission of signals. Christened "information", it will be measured in terms of a fundamental unit called the "bit".

Recognition of this new characteristic brings about a decisive breakthrough. For, as Norbert Wiener describes it, information is neither mass nor energy. In other words, messages and data can be collected without any direct manipulation of matter and with a minute expenditure of energy. What has been discovered here is a completely new dimension of matter.

Data, stored in machines (computers), is structured, "computed" and, after processing, transformed into programmes which, inserted into machines, operate like an automatic control system.

Hitherto, matter had always been processed using energy sources. "Progress" had mobilised more and more powerful sources. Information technologies will use little energy. We are entering a world of reproducibility (e.g. word processing or cloning selected seeds). Technoscience is thus developing completely new technologies, which are interconnected with one another as well as connected to those of the traditional energy sector: informatics, robotics, telecommunications and biotechnologies. The first generation of tools facilitated the production of goods and services in novel ways, generating quantitative growth without creating jobs. The second wave enters a landscape already transformed: computer software, computer-assisted design and production, sensors, electronic mail, interactive imaging, smart cards, etc.

Information technologies are now radically transforming production methods. Even if computerisation and automation directly affect only a small proportion of wage-earners, the breakthrough of service activities and the tertiary sector is drastically altering the job structure in industry as well as the social class structure.

The destabilisation of labour and industry

Technology has destabilised industry, and the market, the globalisation of commerce and the accompanying intensification of competition are adding to the process. Response to modification in demand will have to be almost immediate; even more than coherence and rationality of production, modern industry seeks flexibility, between production units as well. This refashioning of the production system is leading to a radical renewal of the geographical fabric and of employment catchment areas. Information technology is taking on a strategic role in the effort to resist the heightened flow of competition. By organising work in different ways and through the use of information technology, the world of the worker is becoming a "technological" one, integrating the socio-technological environment with the debate in which its subject is already outlined. Thus, over the last few years, we have seen, concomitantly with the exclusion of so many workers, an increase in the power of enterprise projects, "quality circles", and other ways of involving workers in the development of industry.

A "revolution in production" then? The current period is above all one of a new phase in the rationalisation of industry. Strictly speaking, production organised around the interface between volatile demand and programmable automation cannot function within a framework characterised by strict demarcation of the place, role and duties of each participant. But there is a revolution in production in the quest for the ever-increasing integration of new technologies, for a new organisation of work and consequently in the necessity for a new training and manpower management policy.

The concept of integration is becoming fundamental: it requires in turn versatility from certain groups of workers, and hence of those workers' qualifications. On the other hand, the construction of unique information based on a multiplicity of positions, contributions and processing, will act as determinant leading to a redefinition of access to, and validation of, information.

Changes in employment

Jobs are becoming scarce: at point of entry, through the difficulties young people face in attempting to gain "normal" access to gainful work; at point of exit, by large-scale definitive layoffs of so many who could still play an active role. And, in between, numbers of workers experience unemployment of greater or lesser duration, depending on their sex, education level, work experience, the sector of activity, the size of the firm or industry[1] and its position within the fabric of production, the geographical zone, and the local social welfare provision.

The cause of this job rationing is clear. Up to now, all productivity gains encouraged "siphoning off" manpower from sectors in decline into growth sectors; this no longer works. Services, too, are achieving productivity gains.

---

1. While the 1960s were dominated by large-scale firms, it is small and medium businesses which have weathered the crisis best, and which today are believed to have a slightly higher potential for job creation than their larger counterparts.

What is more, in its search for a way out of the crisis, industry has responded with economic and financial restructuring, accompanied by massive layoffs. The very nature of employment is exploding. The individual's career is likely to be sub-divided into a number of segments of various lengths, carrying different levels of status, and with different conditions of social protection and remuneration. Mobility is becoming a dominant characteristic of working life, and calls for different qualifications.

II. Adult education faced with a new social brief

The demand for education influenced by four major challenges

Combating unemployment and the problem of re-integration

One of the most decisive developments in recent years has been the divergence between the world of work and the world of employment. With the growing scarcity of employment, a fine distinction emerges between demands relating to vocational training and demands relating to the statutory form bestowed on the performance of the activity. Work requires skills. It is linked to the technical and organisational choices made, to the practical conditions governing the mobilisation of manpower. It is these needs that vocational training systems cater for.[1]

On the other hand, the crisis has also highlighted the need to tackle two other types of problem which have recently emerged: these are, first, how the individual manages the discontinuous and changing nature of the jobs he does; and second, skills of a more generic kind, which should

---

1. Regardless of the country concerned, systems involving bodies, regulation, financing and administration of vocational training have developed to cater for the needs created by the development of vocational training.

enable individuals, regardless of their level of vocational skill, to be adaptable, flexible, innovative, capable of rapid assimilation into a working community, of rapidly absorbing the written and above all the unwritten rules. In the past it was believed that the more education one has in terms of compulsory schooling — and therefore the more qualifications one has — the more adaptable one is. People are now realising that this assumption will have to be reviewed.

Lastly, it is becoming clear as the end of the century approaches that Europe will no longer be able to create new jobs on the basis of the old systems. It must generate new jobs outside the existing structures and even outside the existing "reservoirs". This can only be achieved by calling upon and mobilising the creativity of individuals, which means that their creativity must be enhanced.

The rising tide of exclusion

When Europe counts its poor by the million, there can be no question of considering exclusion and precariousness as a phenomenon of isolated individuals only.[1]

The processes of exclusion are broader than just deprivation of work. There is no automatic connection between this deprivation and poverty and exclusion. Marginalisation is frequently associated with the development of a defensive, inward-looking culture, linked with the inability of those concerned to change their relationships with the social environment. These phenomena testify to the fact that social ties can become more rigid for certain individuals, certain social groups. This is a constant source of concern to educators: if education cannot be expected to provide a global solution here, we must nevertheless realise what part it plays in producing exclusion.

---

1. Compare, *inter alia*, the studies by ATD-Quart Monde and the report by Father Joseph Wresinski for the Economic and Social Committee.

The task, then, is no longer to help adults to adapt to change, to help them to conform, but also to enable them to acquire the skills and the determination to influence these changes. The role of adult education lies as much in community development as in personal development; such development requires assistance because it implies a re-examination of self, and of one's representations of the environment, and, in more and more cases, this cannot occur spontaneously.

A revolution of socialities

The notion of the "information-based society" purports to signify the invasion of society by symbol and information but even more, the renewal of our everyday landscape; the "new" technologies are modifying the two essential elements in the structuring of our everyday lives — space and time. This essential transformation of modes of exchange leads to a major break with the industrial (and, a fortiori, agricultural) type of society which has culminated since the inter-war period in integrated social worlds, thanks to instruments of social control which themselves have a mass integrating effect.

In these societies, a sense of belonging is today becoming a more important social problem to solve than in the past. Thanks to the penetration of new technologies, among other things, we are no longer in the mass era. Varying in degree from one social group to another, phenomena of tribalisation are developing, of belonging to networks of varying longevity and stability. Social integration suffers here in the expansion or contraction of the social spaces to which people feel they belong, and which vary from one social group to another. More than dualisation, this is a matter of social fragmentation, entailing simultaneously the over-socialisation of some and the de-socialisation of others. Is it not true to say that one of the chief impediments lies in the current problem of the interpenetration of spaces and times? The explosion of the three ages of life, the collapse of the functionality of spaces,[1] the blurring of distinctions between the time allocated to work, leisure and private life,[2] the problems surrounding the interpenetration of cultures etc., are not these examples of dysfunction in the links between social spaces?[3]

Before a solution can be found to the problem of this multiple affiliation, the following questions must first be answered: how can integration in poly-cellular societies be managed? How can worlds which have simply been "stuck together", and vary in stability, be linked together, since they have different organisational systems and dynamics? What can be done to enable individuals to develop a genuine sense of belonging to these different worlds?

A cultural transformation

Already evident in the changes sociality has undergone, the specific nature of the cultural change needs to be defined. As Professor Albert Jacquard pointed out, the 20th century has been one of extraordinary conceptual revolutions: the notions of time, space, entropy, life and so on, have substantially evolved. Yet, in order to express our everyday world, we hang on to expressions and conceptual systems from previous centuries. The new conditions for the formalisation of information are changing our modes of representation: simulation, the use of coded languages and the digitalisation of knowledge are leading to the subordination of meaning and interpretation to calculation. With the progress of information technology, virtuality games are replaced by the ability to programme possible futures. Trapped in a new configuration of the

---

1. The problem of large housing estates is an illustration of this.
2. As regards the new contractual and legislative training measures, of the recent discussion on the notion of "co-investment".
3. Just as the question of minorities and nationalism now highlight the difficulty of formulating problems politically.

media, engaged in a different system of communication, the old intellectual technologies are altering their meaning.

III. Democracy at risk from the fears of an emergent society

The current changes are characterised by their constant acceleration as much as by their unpredictability. The search for identity and its consequences in terms of escape into racism, xenophobia, sectarianism, fundamentalism and extremism, point to an inability to decide where one belongs, to grasp and accept these transitions confronting all countries.[1] All this searching for identity is accompanied by an acute awareness of the vastness of these questions, coupled with an equally acute awareness of the impossibility of understanding them.

Issues concerning genetic manipulation and the development of the environment, for example, place the citizen in a novel situation as compared to the individual whose immediate environment was all he had to comment on. The new potential opened up by scientific developments and their applications mean that individuals have to make choices which, by and large, far exceed their usual horizons as well as their conceptual tools. The growing complexity and interdependence of socio-cultural changes deprive women and men of the tools for understanding these phenomena, and consequently for controlling them.

With the proliferation of information and communication technologies, the explosion of biotechnologies, the restructuring of employment and social welfare systems, the revolution in materials, products and production methods, the formidable growth in mobility both in Europe and

---

1. The consumption of tranquillisers — and other drugs — visits to astrologers and growing interest in the "para-sciences" might also be mentioned in this context.

elsewhere, as well as the resulting linguistic and cultural diversity, a vast range of opportunities is opening up. Societies and individuals are only just beginning to realise their extent. A present is being born, fashioned from uncertainties, for although one may be able to see the negative aspects, its potential benefits are unknown. We live in a world of hyper-choice, into which individuals must be led by the hand and helped. Adult educators are particularly concerned by these major social challenges and by the task of learning to use the new tools implicit in them.

Fragmentation, disintegration, rather than massification, are threatening our societies. This multi-speed socialisation, based on the multiple affiliation of the individual, has to be coped with by individuals. The instruments available are not adequate to the task. The economic crisis as the source of all ills is no longer convincing. In order to provide inspiration for the analyses and proposals which will guide the political choices of the future, it is important to set against the negative, dramatic aspects of dualisation that which is assertive and full of potential. How have the hitherto well-signposted fields of social production become unclear? Which are the areas where the choice for the future lies between progress and social exclusion? The possible emergence of an "information-based society" means that one should not take an over-dramatic view of the present situation, and should envisage the period beyond deregulation as one of transition entailing both obstacles and opportunities.

One of the chief problems calling for priority consideration and solution is the joint management of the market and integration into civil society. In the absence of social cohesion, all hope of growth seems destined to remain vain. This might lead one to question the present ability to deal with the economic, social and cultural aspects separately in order to break the logjam. If the European "model" can have any meaning, it is in the new balance that our societies may be able to achieve between the strengthening of social cohesion — and hence combating exclusion — and the desire to make our economies more productive and efficient.

It is significant in this respect that our societies are now hesitating about the welfare model inherited from the social movements of industrialisation/urbanisation and the compromises they resulted in. Rather than the sort of dependency culture that tends to anaesthetise society, it is significant that numerous voices are calling for greater democracy, greater participation and the involvement of all. This should be understood as meaning a move towards "active societies", societies of responsibility.

In an approach characterised from the very outset by its democratic intentions,[1] what counts is to produce active citizens, who are not merely the product of the differentiation of spaces, but are able to find in them a source of richness and intellectual flexibility. Adult education, in its new definitions and components, must support the individual in his attempt to fashion an identity within a given space, as well as permitting him to move without difficulty from one social space to another.

The strategic role of knowledge

The time when we could think of human instruments as tools for describing an objective reality is long gone. The situation is not one of factual elements conveying determinable meaning on the one hand, and on the other people reacting rationally to these facts. In a period of transition, the important thing is to establish a language, which can properly be called "political", that is, one which "shapes" reality. The primary task of education is not to

---

1. It should be borne in mind that the Council of Europe's primary task, the one that distinguishes it from the phalanx of international intergovernmental organisations, is to promote human rights and pluralist democracy.

produce scholars who can describe the world, but citizens who can build the future. Skills acquired during compulsory school attendance, during childhood and adolescence, can no longer guarantee the flexibility and adaptability required for the whole of one's adult life.

Be they company directors or politicians, they speak with one voice in all the countries of Europe: what is needed is skills insufficiently fostered hitherto, namely flexibility, adaptability, communication skills (listening as much as speaking), the ability to take a stance relative to complex structures and processes. What is true of industry is also true of societies.

The invasion of the multifarious aspects of everyday life by technological advances, the rising level of complexity, the superabundance of information, the transformation of the ensuing socialities and solidarities, the international dimension of the problems arising over the environment, etc., require a redefinition — practical as well as theoretical — of the "social skills" of individuals, so that they can exercise active citizenship.

The need is less for the use of "repeated knowledge", applied on the basis of statistical norms, of rules adopted once and for all — the "wisdom" of the old — and much more for the use of "committed knowledge", in other words, skills which can be learned, implying commitment on the part of the person using them. The major issue now is the possibility of creating skills and expertise that constantly evolve. Motivation, commitment, the ability to learn (and therefore to un-learn), the cumulative nature of access to knowledge, etc. are more fundamental than in a past dominated by Taylorism and the confiscation of knowledge and initiative. The example of the possible creation of new jobs is explicit here.

The assertion that today knowledge is acquiring a strategic value does not just mean that it is becoming more important as a component of new systems of production.

"Knowledge" — in its dual meaning of truth and efficiency — now confronts us with the possibility of *societies of shared intelligence*[1] and is a matter of the organisation of social relations.

This opens up the possibility of *a new social contract* between the requirement of economic efficiency in the use of resources and the demand for freedom in the use of skills. Yet there is nothing inevitable about this. *The building of a new social contract can only be achieved through the development of a new "language", arising from a new approach to socialisation.*

One of the benefits of questioning education and training is their key role, albeit a dual, ambiguous one: at one and the same time positive conditions of access to the information-based society, but also principal causes of the process of exclusion, which are becoming more permanent owing to the cumulative nature of access to knowledge and, in certain respects, more definitive and more comprehensive (exclusion from the job market, from the economic sphere, from relational networks, etc.).

Education is thus acquiring a new and more central function, in proportion to the need for every skill to be constantly maintained and updated if it is to be productive. This both creates and justifies the permanence of the educational function.

IV. A central issue — socialisation

The concept

"Socialisation" means learning and adopting the rules of social exchange. This entails active adaptation, not mere passive absorption, and involves the whole person, who is simultaneously the object and subject of his own sociali-

---

1. Intelligence, not the possession of some ossified, reified expression of knowledge.

sation, and an agent in the socialisation of others. Socialisation therefore aims at overall competence linked with
the individual's exercise of citizenship, his role as a producer of goods and services, and above all as the architect
of his own life.

Education is the major means by which this objective may
be met. It gives individuals the means for understanding
situations, to enable them to form a view and work out
strategies for action.

All of the time-honoured imperatives of education are still
to be found here: the acquisition of culture, of transverse
skills, of experience which can be applied in situations
other than those in which it is learned, of developing
autonomy. The dynamic of this socialising education is
founded on the *"magic triangle"* of development: personal development based on the right to qualifications;
social and economic development; development of citizenship. Seen in this perspective, learning, a lifelong activity, takes on a more precise meaning: it emphasises the
need for adaptability, to be acquired through a constant
input of information,[1] formulation of concepts, exercise of
attitudes and manual skills. Such qualities which are far
more indispensable now than they were in the days of a
relatively static society.

The learning process is not confined to any particular situation or environment. It will give explicit recognition to
the importance of experience that social situations other
than strictly educative ones have enabled the individual to
acquire. Its goal will be to enable the individual to take
stock of his own accumulated experience, to situate it
within a general context, and to assess it in relation to the
various roles he plays in society. It will also organise a life-

---

1. It is clear that the question today is no longer the acquisition of information, but how to discriminate between the various forms of it.

long continuity of study, a cross-fertilisation of experience gained during courses of structured learning alternating with the experience gained through non-structured learning in conjunction with other social activities.

The need to reposition the agencies of socialisation

Thanks to the existence of data banks, information is becoming more and more available in an increasing number of places and circumstances. The nature and volume of information absorbed in daily life through television, newspapers and the performing arts varies a great deal from individual to individual. This mass of accumulated data, impressions and images is snowballing, and it is playing an ever greater role in social segregation.

Over and above the usual economic explanations that used to be found for the crisis, the realisation that there has been a major change in the foundations of the societies we are creating precludes interpreting it as a passing phenomenon. Our societies are being radically reconstituted. The traditional control machinery has lost its relevance. The phenomena of everyday life give rise to fear, bafflement and anxiety.

Adult education must therefore perform a new function. Not only one of social advancement or emancipation, not just one of belated access to the dividends of progress, not that of social reintegration assigned to it in the period of crisis. Its function is to support socialisation on a permanent footing. A kind of adult education now needs to be designed that is capable of providing an effective response to these new requirements.

One of the most significant examples of this redefinition of the concept and role of education is the redefinition of its place in relation to television. Television conveys to its audience, and in so doing creates in them, a culture which to some extent is "universal": it claims universality; its products tend to be the same in all latitudes; in its own special way it combines fiction and advertising, and in so doing conveys a particular way of seeing and conceiving the real and the imaginary; organising moments and events, it both facilitates and prevents insight into meaning and history; it produces the mythologies of modernism.

No definition of adult education (and probably also children's education) can now avoid redefining its practical relationship to televisual and computer-based culture.

Behind their technicality, schemes aiming to encourage integration through an economic approach, enterprise creation, memory training, etc., appear to be linked to ideas of autonomy and participation. Older people, like the most deprived, seek above all to *(re-)establish their social status. In response to this, the training situation should provide a framework in which individual and group problems can be formulated.*

Reinventing education

The social needs that influence the demand for education appear to be inadequately catered for by the present system of supply and demand which emerged through the years of growth and then of crisis.

If the socialisation of individuals becomes permanent, what counts above all is to create the types of back-up it needs. The method of production and distribution of education has to be re-invented, just like the professions which inform it. It is a radical re-examination of what hitherto — indeed since the 18th century — we have considered as the province of childhood and adolescence. It is no longer tenable to believe that an adult, having received basic education, and using the skills furnished by compulsory schooling, will be able to cope with all the ups and downs and novel situations life will deal out. Once one abandons the idea that the individual needs to pursue the infinite path of acquiring knowledge in a developing world, the problem of training arises, and for three main reasons:

- its continuity is part of the related need for social change to develop new modes of operation;
- every situation becomes an educational opportunity (rather than educational reality);
- the educator loses the monopoly as the vehicle of training.

In many countries at present, "adult education" is merely a convenient umbrella term for what is fragmented, scattered, lacking any co-operation or co-ordination concerning policy development, the origin and allocation of resources, the development of programmes and the award of diplomas or certificates. The most one can do is identify *three distinct "sectors"* each of which, in its own way, performs a complementary and largely compensatory role. The most obvious "sector", through the coherence it has everywhere acquired, is that of job-related training primarily intended to supplement full-time school education with specific vocational training. The second covers "general culture" curricula, designed above all to provide access to "culture" for those who have been sidelined early in their school careers. Lastly, and separate from the two sectors just mentioned albeit closely linked to them, there is a range of "second chance" schemes, enabling adults to acquire general knowledge which, in principle, is wholly equivalent to that provided by formal education after the age of compulsory schooling or, in culturally less developed regions, by compulsory schooling.

Given the nature of the questions raised, adult education can no longer stand still. We are back again, not at the watershed of the 1970s but at the origins of the particular social form which was based on the nascent solidarity between industrialisation and democracy; once again we are faced with the demands of modern schooling. It still remains for us to reinvent the education of post-industrial society. The place and status of adult education in that society still has to be defined.

Once the concept of lifelong education had been formulated, it became possible to adopt a set of measures, theories, ideas and practices many of which had predated it, if only in chronological terms. It is therefore important to understand how, in the present conditions, its principles can serve as a basic guide for a relevant response to the demands of the future.

The changes in our societies and the upheavals in our lifestyles confront us with a democratic challenge requiring us to design more suitable responses. Among these, the practical arrangements for a new type of adult education still have to be worked out on the ground. Recent years have been marked above all by growing demands on the adult education system for and by sections of the public which, hitherto, had remained remote from it. Although a response has been given, and with apparent ease, to the need for cultural consumption by the elderly who are now solvent, it remains inadequate, since this need relates to the establishment of the group as a social agency. It is even less adequate where marginalised groups are concerned, who have suffered from long-term exclusion from the world of production, who are poorly educated and have an accumulation of handicaps. Now that the ground has been prepared, continued reference to the principles and methods of lifelong education can be a great help.

The opportunities provided by the new technologies harnessed for use in education still need to be linked up in a proper system, and, by means of greater decentralisation, the broadest possible initiative needs to be made at the local level, at the same time guaranteeing that everyone has the opportunity for training throughout life to meet the situations and the needs that will arise.

Constructing learning situations within a coherent, co-ordinated education system

In any discussion on the adult education of tomorrow, there are two factors that need to be tackled together; the social urgency of responding to the needs of the most disadvantaged groups and becoming part of the "information society". Faced with this twofold requirement, while the "adult education and social change" project has confirmed the illusory nature of an "educative society",[1] it has also shown that there must be a formal break with the concept of lifelong education as a system but naturally not as a method! In other words, the aim is not to devise a comprehensive institutionalised education system, from

---

1. The case of the long-term unemployed is but one illustration of the fact that society is not directly educational. Although the role of the educational component in the context of social work changes, it still remains a specific function.

infancy to death. What is needed is to construct a coherent system able permanently to perform a support function for the socialisation of individuals as members of a community.

It is not a question of organising short-term responses to re-qualify individuals to take on a job, but rather of improving their motivation and their real chances of exercising their skills on the job market;[1] of extending the instructor's brief to include social skills, notably the ability to see oneself as an active subject with a right to full exercise of citizenship.

I. Three dimensions for reconstruction

A new "culture"

We must assume the continuing unpredictability of the future. New demands and new ways of doing things require a different kind of knowledge, and call for the creation of a veritable "culture of uncertainty". Developing receptivity to the creative demands a complete overhaul of our attitudes, a fundamental rethink on the learning processes which form them. The insecurity being experienced by the majority of people stems from our refusal to relativise knowledge and values. New demands and new ways of doing things require a different kind of knowledge, a different understanding, often described as "systemic". This is all the more necessary in that our approach to reality in terms of uncertainty is not limited to the cognitive plane, but also falls within the sphere of the sensate and the relational. Developing receptivity to the creative calls for a transformation of our culture, a complete transformation in our attitudes and a re-examination of the educational process leading to them.

---

1. The unemployed person's first priority is to find a job.

Information is not training. What matters is not so much the volume of the information as the ability to apply it. Intelligence is not a question of access to infinite quantities of possibilities, but is to be used in selecting among them. Thinking is the modification of one's perceptions, the invention of new distinctions, new indexes to be used as a basis for reconstituting reality, formulating new axioms, modifying one's perceptions, perceiving a message where one had at first been aware only of noise, bringing new meaning into focus. The power of a concept is proportionate to its capacity to extract itself from established parameters, to give rise to unanticipated networks of relevance.

A strategic concept: employability

Faced with the non-applicability of established policies, states have increased their specialised measures targeted on job creation to offset the impact of recession on unskilled workers. Based on the idea that a gap exists between the qualifications people have and those required on the job market, these measures strive to "flexibilise" the training process in order to respond to market demands, in close collaboration with employers and with workers' representatives.

Associated with the concepts of integration into the world of work and social "and" vocational reintegration (though the nature of this link is not clearly defined) and of new forms of integration into employment, implementation of these measures has brought out a new field of social practice, with a particular impact on both the theory and practice of training.

It is not the difficulty of placement which constitutes the novelty here, but the opening up of an institutional field of work in the time-suspension of "active inactivity". The notion of employability responds to the necessity of forging a specific terminology reflecting the new employment situation which is neither part of the productive system, nor yet social assistance. The question, though, is to ascertain whether the term should be applied to a given individual, or to his environment: how it is that a worker who was "employable" yesterday becomes "unemployable" the moment he is made redundant.

In fact, employability is an ambiguous concept. At one level, it is sufficiently fluid to allow for compromise between actors, and sufficiently polysemous to warrant different logical approaches and applications. Moreover, it objectifies and personalises — more than it individualises — one's "chances" of reclassification. On another level, it brings together two elements which do not belong to the same logical order, namely the objective reality of reduced opportunity, and the subjective experience of discouragement: the only real issue, when looking for work, is finding and getting a job.

From this point of view, "employability" reproduces the ambiguity characteristic of qualifications generally, between the post to be filled and the individual filling it; but it shifts the focus from the field of work to that of employment. In consequence, it legitimises the involvement of educators in a distinct field of training, namely, vocational training organised in direct consultation with industry.

Employability and qualification, while not mutually exclusive, do justify the implementation of two distinct training systems. Part of this system is based more directly on the new approach to action: to enable participants to overcome handicaps (cultural and relational shortfalls) and to develop a programme of social and vocational reintegration based on the acquisition of experience. The areas addressed by this approach cover three dimensions: the first, linked to exclusion from work; the other two, corresponding to a lack of "capital" in the relational and cultural spheres, which in turn determine one's ability to engage in an activity, to develop a social identity, to participate normally in a social community.

This repositioning opens up a practical alternative at the very moment when the need for redeployment, which is often dramatic and always concerns massive numbers of people, cannot, because of the shortage of jobs, find expression in terms of employment. Accompanied by the emergence of a new and diffuse notion — that of *basic competence* — and of a tool which appears to render it operational — *cognitive aptitude* — it enables educators to reinvest the existing body of aptitudes, skills and behaviours which, without excluding those relevant to the world of work, cannot be reduced to such limited dimensions. This approach to education is not put forward merely in order to raise the qualification level of the population in general, nor to meet a simple need for culture and activity on the part of the unemployed. This approach, far from entailing an exercise in catching up or rectifying damage, is a complete change of direction.

Priority access

The question of access, which has become a priority, cannot therefore be solved solely within the parameters of education. Obstacles of all kinds stand in the way: previous failures and negative social image, unsuitability and rigidity of curricula, difficulties of physical access, geographical or cultural distance, selection processes, having to pay, children to look after, and so forth. Socially, education is a secondary activity for the most disadvantaged persons too — and perhaps above all for them. This being so, to re-establish education as a full and complete activity is a comprehensive task in which all those who are engaged in education should participate. Improving access for all must be subject to positive discrimination in favour of adults with the greatest difficulties.

II. A fundamental reconsideration of educational engineering

A system of opportunities for learning throughout life, in a wide variety of situations and institutions within school and outside it, has still to be developed; it should be organised and coherent, open to all, and influenced by all. This means an extensive overhaul of education within its environment at the same time as a change in the education provided.

Political determination alone will make possible this large-scale reform, centred on and close to the learner, so that individuals can be offered a service for developing an educational programme, designing personalised courses within a range of learning situations and recognising experience. Five new strategies can be identified in this area.

Individualising

The aim here is to make the adult the agent of his own training. There is no such thing as a model trainee. Every adult has his own history, skills, learning rhythm, not to mention his perceptions and values, which form the basis of his spontaneous evaluations of his surroundings and experience. An analysis of demand, inseparable from motivation, and never spontaneous or precise, is central. The work in question is one of transformation, beginning with a vague, diffuse, multidimensional approach.

The purpose of this type of education is less to facilitate access to existing knowledge than to promote and enrich the experience of every adult, to enable him to learn to fit in, to learn how to learn, to identify his existing skills and knowledge, to become capable of transferring them to new situations. What counts is the capacity to cope with changing circumstances, from the most private to the most communal. The dimension which must not be lost sight of is that of capitalising on experience. More importance must be attached to raising awareness and sensitivity to

130

new realities, to developing the ability to critically evaluate change and develop original forms of personal and collective behaviour, to develop motivation, the will to surmount difficulties, and the self-confidence to do so.

The novelty of this approach is its rejection of the concept of training as a moment of preparation, to be undertaken prior to any "practical" application, and by definition before gaining access to employment. We add our voices to those of the people involved in the Helmond Project in the Netherlands in arguing for a shift of concept: training, far from being synonymous with preparation for that which the learner will be doing tomorrow — which in any case may well be obsolete by then — must be synonymous with opening up, with developing what the individual is, and does, today. Education should not be consigned to a place of chronological antecedence: it should instead be recognised as properly belonging to the functions of construction, deployment, empowering.

This approach, underpinned by the new technological opportunities, leads to a view of education as a permanent process of development, affecting all the emotional, physical and intellectual capacities of women and men, their memory and imagination, their sense of difference and community, their aptitudes for fitting in, acting, learning, and so on.

Essentially, where pedagogical methods are concerned, we here remain within the main lines of the successive Council of Europe adult education projects, one of the chief aims of which has been to bring learners closer to educational services and programmes, in other words to adapt education to the needs, aspirations and motivations of would-be learners. In particular, the idea of analysing needs is further corroborated by the desire to individualise, which remains the principal achievement of this project.

Individualisation, presented as a measure which reinforces the effectiveness of active education, taking into account the project of the individual and basing itself on his experience, existing abilities and potential, entails profound changes in:

- the pre-training phase: the practice of personal and/or vocational stocktaking, situating the learner in relation to an educational benchmark, assistance with creating and managing a personal project, etc.;

- the training phase itself: educational programme, modular training, varied teaching, guided independence, self-training, etc.;

- the post-training phase: the practice of evaluation, the search for validation, improving follow-up, etc.

The desire to start with the learner, with his experience and objectives, makes the following functions indispensable:

- individualised help and guidance to assist learners to construct a project and arrange a specially adapted, personalised course of study;

- information, reception, help/guidance, thus underpinning the commitment to the educational process with genuine "negotiation";

- support: precariousness precludes education: the problems — financial and legal, housing and health, alcoholism and drugs, etc. — which prevent the learner from fully participating in his training must be dealt with individually;

- facilitating access for all adults by providing various services (crèches, transport facilities, etc.).

The purpose is to give the individual the means to control his learning activity, the development of his own particular course of study and the assessment of the skills learned, by selecting what he needs from the range of educational opportunities available and determining his own progress and learning rate. The learning process is the engine of pedagogical engineering, the purpose of which is to *create specific educational situations*. A situation is not educational by virtue of its institutional character in school. None the less, while any educational situation is potentially formative in itself, it is not genuinely so until after the process of organisation. Also, every individual can learn, providing his own action and learning requirements are respected.

Diversifying supply

The aim is in no sense to sweep aside existing arrangements and systems, but to find a different way of linking and integrating them into a true, more complex and richer education system in which adult education will find its full, coherent realisation.

The idea of the personalised course of study assumes that the individual is at all times in a continuum consisting of initial training, vocational integration, social experience, vocational experience and recurrent periods of further training. What the project does is to identify the various functions performed by the different aspects of supply and to point the way to a more rational whole, provided the bolts separating them into compartments are sprung.

One key factor in the continuum is the need to create a coherent structure encompassing the various opportunities for learning and acquiring skills, in such a way that avenues and bridges exist between the various courses. Pluralism of supply must therefore be promoted by encouraging the development of organisational networks. A network-based organisation preserving the autonomy of the various segments will facilitate the development of paths of development that are both vertical and horizontal.

There has been such an acceleration in technological progress, with new knowledge and skills requiring instant application, that there is no longer time for an intermediate stage: a constantly changing situation requires a constantly changing response, and needs must be addressed as and when they arise. The interplay between the world of work and the education system is modified by this development. School is not the only place where it is possible to gain access to new knowledge. On the other hand, it is the only place where it is possible to learn, in other words to work on one's representations and experience. Seen as a *service*, to be developed with the collaboration of all concerned, and with due regard for the interests of each, education faces challenges which by definition *planning* cannot begin to address.

Co-ordinating the system (networks and partnerships)

In the same manner as for vocational training formerly, the time has now come for a co-ordinated adult education policy. The priority is to gather together in a coherent system what today is disparate and fragmented, in order to construct a type of education geared to the need for the democratic construction of an "information-based" society so that new types of social and vocational integration can be found.

The classic approach to education faces its main challenges at the programming and planning stages. The central role of planning in the classic approach was justified by the characteristics of that approach, namely, unity of content, shared goals (preparing learners for work in the industrial system of production) and the separation of the school from other social functions. The new approach places less emphasis on planning and more on co-ordination based on a practice in which educational engineering is the determinant.

By stressing the decentralisation of initiative, we hope to attain a better balance between centralisation and decentralisation. In a trend analogous to that in production structures, much positive empirical evidence favours a co-ordinated system of small centres close to the communities they serve, over the more centralised, larger-scale approach.

This rapprochement encourages material access (by using existing infrastructures), participation and recourse to instructors drawn from the community itself, speaking the same language and experiencing identical problems. Yet flexibility is not synonymous with atomisation. Unregulated decentralisation would exacerbate existing regional or local inequalities, because of on-the-spot variations in availability of resources. Educational supply must be seen in terms of redistribution in accordance with a policy aimed at establishing greater equality.

In this way, the process of breaking monolithic organisational structures into smaller local units simultaneously develops the concept of combining these in new ways: this prospect is in turn linked, through the perspective of evaluation, with the mechanism of unit-credits. A system conceived on such a scale gives rise to a need for new rules of management and ways of functioning.

This *multi-partnership* obliges each operative to enter into increased contact and liaison with more, and above all more diversified, partners, with different approaches; these links cannot be neatly codified. It is the purpose of the network to order action while maintaining flexibility: through processing data and making as much as possible available; by seeking co-operation with other institutions and through co-ordination.

The spatial reorganisation of cultural/educational supply is indispensable if the inequalities of dispersion and geographical remoteness are to be remedied. Yet essentially the system will not be renewed by the use of the "new educational technologies", even though this may provide a partial solution. Multi-faceted education, the "search for the best combination of all methods of teaching and communication" is preferable to the "multi-media approach" which is today exerting an unwarranted attraction.

The current fragmentation of skills and responsibilities is quite counterproductive. There is evidence of a quite widespread tendency among states to off-load their responsibility on to other partners: counties, municipalities, private operators, even voluntary contributions by participants. As things stand, these choices lead to the marginalisation of this activity relative to other administrative sectors and to recourse in the worst cases, to voluntary work.

Adult education must be regulated as part of a coherent whole. One urgent task is to identify and bring together all those concerned. The experiments described have revealed the importance of encouragement and support from local communities as well as the social partners. It is important in this connection:

– to re-territorialise, in other words to make education a component of projects implemented by a whole territorial community, encompassing all aspects of concerted development. It is through measures of this kind, rooted in the areas directly concerned and in the social fabric as a whole, that the educational supply will become truly accessible, close at hand and socially useful;

– to ensure, at local level, co-operation among all the educational, social and cultural components. For example, it will be for the local authorities to base the development of the learning supply on negotiation among all the partners; to organise operational and co-operative co-ordination between the administrative departments responsible for the different levels of adult education, in order to prevent duplication; to ensure a more realistic distribution of resources, more efficient organisation and communication and the dissemination of innovations as well as the identification of needs not catered for.

Professionalising the operators

The reconstruction of education depends on educators. The current diversification of the function of education is leading to both internal collapse and to a redefinition of the frontiers with other occupations. The operators' traditional role was as transmitters or distributors of formal knowledge. Today, they are being asked to work as the architects or designers of education; as assemblers, as engineers in the implementation of complex systems; as counsellors, guides, evaluators. The educator's brief is broadening to incorporate functions which have nothing to do with organisation *per se*, into the act of providing education.

Two key functions emerge in connection with this changeover: the educator as engineer, and as guide and adviser. Educational engineering is a new demand on the educator, requiring him to spot problems and to construct appropriate educative responses. This task calls for the construction of tools and approaches specific to each situation. As for facilitation, it is characterised by a certain diversity. Without relinquishing his *function of imparting knowledge* (but sharing this function with others), the educator's role will be divided between an organisational function (encouraging expression, identifying needs), and one of tracing progress and maintaining awareness with regard to the objectives defined in the framework of "contract pedagogy",[1] as well as an evaluative function.

One of the strong elements in recent years has been the realisation that educators are undergoing a twofold evolution:

- on the one hand, their functions are broadening in scope; in other words, the functions of reception, of assessing skills, of guidance and direction, etc. are now grafted on to the traditional function of transmitting knowledge;

- on the other hand, this function is opening up to "non-professionals". Voluntary associations form a crucial link in the expression and formulation of the felt needs of local people, and identifying projects which could incorporate an educative role. Nonetheless, this link must be properly organised. Voluntary involvement should be encouraged, provided that the terms of collaboration are clearly spelled out, including clear specifications re professional requirements and the nature of involvement. Often goodwill — or even militarism — must stop up the gaps arising from lack of professionalism. Energy, enthusiasm, charisma, while all important qualities with a real input to adult education, are not transferable. Transferability can only be conveyed through a professional approach.

Teaching — instructing, communicating knowledge — cannot be improvised. Competence and responsibility are

---

1. In connection with this subject, we note the suggestion of Father Liam Carey, for whom the concept of "tutor" expresses all of these functions. According to him, the tutor is first and foremost a counsellor whose function is to identify problems. He is also a leader in the sense of galvanising group dynamics in order to reinforce motivation, and a resource-person with co-ordinating role (putting learners in touch with each other, and with new equipment and skills); as well as being called upon to mobilise different strategies in facilitating the progress of individuals and group; finally he must be able to evaluate. One of the essential functions of the tutor is to create the group as a collective entity, for this transformation is not a spontaneous phenomenon, and must on the contrary be developed through controlled activity.

to be achieved through a precise approach. This results in a twofold obligation:

– professionalising the hard core of educators responsible for managing the system, ensuring it is consistent, negotiating individual courses of study and consolidating and guaranteeing the quality of the educational facilities provided;

– improving the skills of "non-professionals" involved in educational action.

Establishing legal guarantees and stable funding

Restructuring adult education requires two complementary aspects in order to guarantee the protection of minorities and offset inequalities through positive discrimination:

– on the one hand, modernising the educational supply. The growth of demand is accompanied by the impossibility for public finance to increase in like measure. Adult education must therefore change its methods of production and distribution to achieve better quality while reducing unit costs. It has been shown that recourse to the opportunities offered by new technologies remains limited at present. Also, the hypothesis of a *systematic obligation to produce results* will help to strengthen a number of systems, and, in particular, to provide a comparative assessment of the logic of financing projects and the individual logic of "coupons" or "education/ training vouchers";

– on the other hand, it is necessary to offer legal guarantees other than those offered by the "right to adult education" which currently exists in the countries of western Europe, which is more "moral" than legal and more centred on employment and vocational qualification, to the detriment of "community" skills. The crucial element in renovating the right to adult education today concerns the quality of the laws that make it possible to define the right to education as a right analogous to that secured to children; a right of the adult individual to access, throughout life, to quality education regardless of age, sex, membership of a particular ethnic or linguistic group, social, marital or professional status, the presence of handicaps or financial situation.

Concluding comments: combating exclusion and entering the information society

It is a worthwhile exercise today to take stock of the changes which have occurred since the 1960s. The cultural humanism of the pioneers of permanent education has had its day. The crisis put an end to that burst of enthusiasm. Educators found themselves confronted by the need to support action, to forge new tools. This experience was decisive. Guided by the aims of the permanent education project, its principles were heavily pruned to meet the requirements and constraints of development. Our world did not become — far from it — one of leisure and the society of abundance. Tensions have built up. Jobs are scarce and social welfare systems seriously destabilised. The meaning and direction of work are changing. Europe has once again become a place of conflict. Destitution and precariousness are the common fate of large sections of society. The demographic outlook for the near future is alarming. Fighting Aids or struggling to save the planet have little in common with celebrating the millennium.

A world is emerging. Mass societies are giving way to relatively stable associations of cultural groups which themselves have been weakened, to associations of more ephemeral networks of allegiance. Does this mean that our future will be tribalistic? How can the idea of pluralist democracy be protected from the current proliferation of messianic ideologues, who encourage people not to think, but to seek refuge in the most illusory beliefs? How can exclusion be combated? How can one deal with the things which foster racism, delinquency, xenophobia and the temptations of totalitarianism? These questions imply opting for responsibility in order to arbitrate the present in the name of the future. In planning his potential futures, the human being finds himself confronted with himself. Hence the enormous anxiety about what he is, about his guiding principles, and about the environment which has fashioned him. Even if the long-term choices conflict with immediate interests, the social groups affected by such issues must be made to discuss them.

It is a matter of managing transition. With the cohesion of its social fabric and democratic structures under threat, Europe is confronted by the necessity to *collectively* create new machinery for production and social control as well as the bodies to operate this machinery. The extent of these changes is largely unknown. No one can predict the level to which artificial intelligence will be able to raise machine performance. New equilibria, new social contracts must be created, in industry, family, urban areas and regions. Finding urgent, practical and lasting solutions to the task of inventing new types of social and vocational integration means that adult education must be viewed as a *political issue* (the promotion of pluralist democracy and human rights), as well as an economic one (the development of competitiveness, productivity and performance in the area of quality).

There is still a need to mould responsible citizens. Political freedom can no longer be defined as the freedom to express one's opinion. The increasingly fundamental problem is the process of shaping this opinion. Democracy is a choice. Implementing it requires an effort on our part. This being so, neither the consumption of the products of culture, nor social advancement, nor even simply vocational qualifications are on the agenda any more. The changes are revealing a range of educational needs around what we have analysed as "social" or "community skills". To be compatible with the choice of democracy, adult education must play a fundamental role in building democratic structures and establishing human rights in societies founded on a new role for knowledge. It must enable every person to participate fully in the process of determining the choices which shape his destiny and to become an active agent of development.

A field is opening up. Educators must look towards new horizons. Close examination reveals that education now has to deal with questions it first encountered at the inception of the modern school, at a time when industrialisation and democracy were developing. It is our job to invent the education of the post-industrial society and to define the place and status of adult education within it. The demands being made of education today are ambitious with regard to the numbers of people concerned and the nature of the fields to be covered. Unless we want to choose dualisation, we must — as swiftly and as broadly as possible — make up for lost time, not only with regard to technological advances but also the destructuration of thought, personality and whole social groups; handicaps in all these areas are mounting. In the climate of uncertainty regarding what will prove necessary, a policy of over-investment in knowledge is inseparable from our gamble on the future.

Bibliography

1. Education permanente, recueil d'études comman-ditées par le Conseil de la coopération culturelle. Une contribution à "l'Année internationale de l'éduca-tion" des Nations Unies. Strasbourg, 1970.

2. Education permanente, synopsis de 15 études. Stras-bourg, February 1971. CCC/EES(70) 133.

3. Education permanente, Fondements d'une politique éducative intégrée. François Lebouteux. Strasbourg, October 1971. 21/1971.

4. Education permanente, principes de base. Stras-bourg, 1973.

5. Le métier de formateur. Typologie des formateurs d'adultes. J-J Scheffknecht. Strasbourg, 1975. [3927]

6. L'éducation permanente, un cadre pour l'éducation récurrente: théorie et pratique. Rapport analytique présenté par le Secrétariat du Conseil de l'Europe. Conférence permanente des Ministres européens de l'Education. Stockholm, June 1975.

7. Organisation, contenu et méthodes de l'éducation des adultes. Présenté par le directeur de projet, Henri Janne. Strasbourg, 1977. CCC/EES (77) 3.

8. Structures organiques et territoriales de l'éducation des adultes. Strasbourg, 1979.

9. Education des adultes, emploi et groupes défavorisés. Strasbourg, 1979.

10. Actualité d'une politique d'éducation permanente. "Le programme de Sienne". J-J Scheffknecht. Stras-bourg, 1980. DECS-EES/ EP (79) 3 Definitive.

11. Développement de l'éducation des adultes. Rapport

final du projet No. 3 du CDCC "Développement de l'éducation des adultes", par Henri Janne, Pierre Dominice et Walter James. Strasbourg, 1980.

12. Développement, politique régionale de formation et éducation des adultes. J-J Scheffknecht. Strasbourg, 1982. 41 p. [3926].

13. Contribution au développement d'une nouvelle politique éducative. Strasbourg, 1982.

14. Project No. 9 — Adult education and community development. 6 000 days in front of us: new and old employment and unemployment in perspective. By Saverio Avveduto. Strasbourg, 1985.

15. Project No. 9 — Adult education and community development. Summary comprising action proposals for the implementation of integrated development projects. Strasbourg, 1985.

16. Project No. 9 — Adult education and community development. Some conclusions from the co-operation of fourteen development projects. By Walter James. Strasbourg, 1985.

17. Project No. 9 — Adult education and community development. The fourteen pilot experiments. Volume 1: Participation of men and women in decisions affecting their daily life on a wide range of local and regional issues. Switzerland, Spain, Portugal, Italy. Strasbourg, 1985.

18. Project No. 9 — Adult education and community development. The fourteen pilot experiments. Volume 2: Responses to unemployment and to the consequences of economic restructuring. Finland, Belgium, Sweden, Denmark, Federal Republic of Germany, France. Strasbourg, 1985.

19. Project No. 9 — Adult education and community development. The fourteen pilot experiments.

Volume 3: Co-operative development group No. 3 "Evolution of the social and cultural roles of women and men". Netherlands, United Kingdom, Turkey, Norway. Strasbourg, 1985.

20. Project No. 9 — Adult education and community development. Comments and illustrations by Christian Darvogne. Strasbourg, 1986. CC/GP9 (85) 14.

21. Project No. 9 — Adult education and community development. Responses to unemployment in the context of local and regional development. Hofgeismar Seminar (24-26 April 1985). Strasbourg, 1986.

22. Project No. 9 — Adult education and community development. Development project networks: Scope for implementation in Spain and Italy. By José Antonio Fernandez and Marcello Limina. Strasbourg, 1986.

23. Project No. 9 — Adult education and community development. Social movements and adult education. Brussels Seminar (6-8 May 1985). Strasbourg, 1986.

24. Project No. 9 — Adult education and community development. Changes in working life: opportunities for learning? Landskrona Seminar (11-14 June 1985). Strasbourg, 1986.

25. Project No. 9 — Adult education and community development. From rigidity to flexibility: work, education, social relations. By Henri Janne. Strasbourg, 1986.

26. Project No. 9 — Adult education and community relations. Avila Seminar (2-5 July 1985). Strasbourg, 1986.

27. Project No. 9 — Adult education and community development: Responses to unemployment and the

147

consequences of economic restructuring. Chislehurst Seminar. (23-26 July 1985). Strasbourg, 1986.

28. Project No. 9 — Adult education and community development. Local development as a factor of social innovation and economic productivity. Sèvres Seminar (17-19 September 1985). Strasbourg, 1985.

29. Project No. 9 — Adult education and community development. Strasbourg, 1987.

30. Project No. 9 — Conference on "Adult Education and Community Development — Challenge and Response". Strasbourg, 26-29 May 1986. Summary report by Hugues de Jouvenel. 1987.

31. Adult Education and Social Change. Interim report (1989-90). By Gérald Bogard. Strasbourg, 1991.

32. La lutte contre l'intolérance et la xénophobie dans les activités du Conseil de l'Europe. By Antonio Perotti. Strasbourg, 1989.

33. De nouveaux minoritaires dans la cité européenne. Conférence pluridisciplinaire sur les aspects éducatifs et culturels des relations intercommunautaires. Strasbourg, 5-7 December 1989. General report by Jacques Berque. 1991.

34. Les qualifications-clés aux stades initial et ultérieur de la formation. Identification et mode d'acquisition de qualités ou qualifications-clé aux stades initial et ultérieur de la formation. Dieter Mertens. CCC/EES (72) 110.

35. La formation et le recyclage des éducateurs d'adultes. Albert Pflüger. CDCC. Strasbourg, 1978.

36. Les chômeurs pigés par le chômage. Enlisement dans le chômage et faible scolarisation dans quelques pays. — Belgium, France, Portugal, Spain, Sweden, United Kingdom. Mateo Alaluf. CDCC 1992.

37. La coordination des services publics dans les domaines social, de l'emploi et de l'éducation pour l'insertion ou la réinsertion professionnelle des personnes en difficulté. Francis Bailleau. CDE. 1992.

38. Christian Charpy. Etude préliminaire sur le chômage de longue durée en Europe. DECS/EES (88) 6.

39. Le réseau des initiatives pour l'éducation des adultes et le développement communautaire. Escorial Seminar organised by the Spanish Ministry of National Education. 24-26 April 1989. Council of Europe DECS/AE (91) 16.

40. Colloquy. Vers une plus grande justice sociale en Europe: le défi de la marginalisation et de la pauvreté. Strasbourg, 3-5 December 1991. Actes. Steering Committee on Social Policy

41. Chômeurs de longue durée et personnes âgés au sein des migrants en Europe. Jagdish Gundara and Crispin Jones. Strasbourg, 1992.

42. Adult education and social change. Report of the Belgrade Conference. Strasbourg, 1992.

43. Pour une éducation socialisatrice. Constituer l'éducation en système autonome. Rapport d'orientation. Gérald Bogard. Strasbourg, 1992.

44. Towards an active, responsible citizenship. Adult education to counter exclusion and to guide the process of social change. Final project report "Adult education and social change". Gérald Bogard. Strasbourg, DECS/AE (93) 6 — 1993.

45. Adult education in member countries. Peter Clyne. DECS/AE (93) 9. Strasbourg, 1993.

46. Le rôle des services de l'emploi et de formation dans la lutte contre le chômage de longue durée. Strasbourg, 1992.

47. Growing old differently? DECS/AE (93) 8. Gérald Bogard and William Tyler. Strasbourg, 1993.

48. Adult education at the Council of Europe. Etapes d'un projet. Gérald Bogard. Strasbourg, 1992.

49. Les gens, l'apprentissage et les métiers: l'éducation des adultes et les chômeurs de longue durée. Lancaster. 25-28 September 1990. Strasbourg, 1991.

50. La lutte contre l'intolérance et la xénophobie dans les activités du Conseil de l'Europe 1969-1989. Antonio Perotti. Strasbourg, 1991.

51. Modernisation sans exclusion. Rapport de la Conférence finale du projet "Adult education and social change". Strasbourg, May 1993. Gérald Bogard (to be published).

Appendix I: The Council for Cultural Co-operation

An instrument of cultural co-operation at the Council of Europe, the Council for Cultural Co-operation (CCC) was set up on 1 January 1962 by the Committee of Ministers. It was allocated a threefold role:

- to formulate proposals concerning the Council's cultural policy;

- to co-ordinate and implement the Organisation's entire cultural programme; and

- to apportion the resources of the Cultural Fund (thus conferring administrative and budgetary autonomy on it).

At that time, the CCC was composed of one delegation from each government, three members of the Parliamentary Assembly, four representatives from the European Cultural Foundation and lastly, the chairmen of the three standing committees; of the latter, made up of senior officials, one is responsible for higher education and research, one for general and technical education and one for out-of-school education and cultural development. All the member governments of the Council of Europe,[1] as well as the signatories to the European Cultural Convention[2] are represented on these bodies.

In the field of education, the aim of the Council for Cultural Co-operation is to help provide young Europeans, regardless of their origins or intellectual standard, with suitable educational opportunities and help them adapt to

---

1. In 1973 these were Austria, Belgium, Cyprus, Denmark, France, Ireland, Iceland, Italy, Luxembourg, Malta, Norway, Netherlands, Federal Republic of Germany, United Kingdom, Sweden, Switzerland and Turkey.
2. Greece, Spain, Finland and the Holy See.

political and social change. All matters with a bearing on the acquisition of knowledge are studied, ranging from television in the home, the organisation of youth centres, and improving teacher training to advanced research. In this way, every European state is expected to be able to take advantage of the experience of the others in planning and structural reform, curricula and methods in the various branches of education. Naturally, adult education was dealt with by the Directorate of Education in what was then the Division for Out-of-School Education.

The doctrine of the Council of Europe

It is not possible to set guidelines for an adult education policy in the member countries of the Council of Europe without referring to the political objectives which were laid down for this international organisation. The Statute of the Council of Europe, and a number of basic texts adopted since it was created, concerning such fundamental concepts as democracy, human rights, including freedom of thought and expression, economic, social and cultural rights as well as the right to education, enable us to define a framework within which an adult education policy could be designed, targeted and implemented in the member states.

The Statute of the Council of Europe emphasises that the governments of member states are unshakeably attached "to the spiritual and moral values which are the common heritage of their peoples and the true source of individual freedom, political liberty and the rule of law, principles which form the basis of all genuine democracy." (Preamble, paragraph 3).

One of the political objectives of the Council is "to achieve a closer unity between its members ... by agreements and common action", particularly where "the maintenance and further realisation of human rights and fundamental freedoms" is concerned. (Article 1 of the Statute).

The governments of the member states also recognise the principle "of the enjoyment by all persons within [their] jurisdiction of human rights and fundamental freedoms" (Article 3 of the Statute).

The most important achievement of the Council of Europe has without a doubt been the conclusion and implementation of the Convention for the Protection of Human Rights and Fundamental Freedoms (generally known as the European Convention on Human Rights) and its five additional protocols. The convention is supplemented by the European Social Charter, an instrument which aims to guarantee a number of social rights.

The adoption by the Committee of Ministers of the Council of Europe of the Declaration on Human Rights on 27 April 1978 confirms the Council of Europe's vocation in the protection and promotion of human rights and fundamental freedoms. In this Declaration, the governments of the member states reaffirmed the importance of the European Convention on Human Rights in the international protection of these rights and their effective exercise in Europe. They decided to give priority to new moves to extend the lists of individual rights, in particular rights in the social, economic and cultural fields, which ought to be protected by European conventions or other appropriate means. And they undertook to participate actively in the protection and promotion of human rights and fundamental freedoms including, in a wider sense, rights falling within the social, economic and cultural fields, thereby contributing to the strengthening of world peace and security and international co-operation as well as the economic and social progress of all peoples.

In parallel with this, and as a response to the initiatives taken by the Committee of Ministers, the Parliamentary Assembly adopted two recommendations on, respectively, widening the scope of the European Convention on Human Rights and revision of the European Social Charter. In addition to the right to education stipulated in the first Protocol to the Convention, the Assembly proposed the inclusion and broadening of certain social rights, such as those relating to "access to free employment services, vocational guidance and vocational training" and made it clear that the right "must be fundamental and enjoy general recognition, and capable of sufficiently precise definition to lay legal obligations on a state, rather than simply constitute a general rule" (Recommendation 838 (1978)). The Assembly passed a second recommendation to update certain standards and include "new rights", such as the "right to education, particularly basic education and the right to educational leave" in the European Social Charter. (Recommendation 839 (1978)).

Some ten years after the implementation of the European Cultural Convention, and more particularly in the field of education, a text on the Council of Europe's cultural policy, adopted in 1965 by the Committee of Ministers, stipulates that one of the "primary objectives of European cultural co-operation is to draw the attention of all members to the new ideas, technologies and achievements of any one of them and to facilitate their adaptation to the needs of all of them [...] The purpose of these measures will not only be to increase the educational potential of every nation, but also to develop mutual aid between nations and increase the number of instruments for practical co-operation between European educators".

Since the Human Rights Declaration of 1978, various Council of Europe bodies have been working to develop higher standards for the economic, social and cultural rights of individuals and groups, as well as the obligations these place on member states.

154

The Council of Europe's method:

Co-operative development

The approach of the Council of Europe in this area is an original one, based as it is on study visits and specific projects, interspersed with meetings with the designers, the "educational engineers" and the beneficiaries of these measures.

"The originality of the method adopted by the Steering Group is worth emphasising. The fact that the study and evaluation of national innovations should have been conducted on the basis of a common philosophy not only has intrinsic merit, but also permits a "retroactive" appraisal in two ways: the concept of permanent education and the methods of implementing it (attaching particular importance to those involving the principle of recurrence) can be clarified and refined even further in the light of the information drawn from experiments, the modified concept in turn producing amended criteria for the choice of future experiments. This dialectical process of measuring the concept against the reality is therefore destined to be continuous and to self-enriching, to lead us both to growing coherence in and between the various branches of education and towards European harmonisation, once it has proved possible to generalise it to the point where it can be made into a large-scale co-operative enterprise." (6/2)

The advantages of the co-operative development method

The method adopted in recent adult education projects was significant, for it imparted fresh meaning and a fresh dimension to international co-operation for European solidarity. Notwithstanding the wide diversity and divergence of cultural, economic, social and political contexts and traditions, the problems were similar, or at least comparable,

155

in the various regions of Europe. There were convergent approaches and experiments between initiatives geographically remote from one another, endeavouring to respond to the new challenges created by the crisis in Europe today.

This method has:

- established and stepped up contacts between decision-makers, field workers and experts, and supported their mutual involvement in activities;

- made it possible to create not merely a system for exchanging information, experience and ideas, but regular cross-fertilisation between experiments themselves, thereby becoming a process of active co-operation, in which those responsible work together to formulate joint proposals for future action;

- developed to the point where it has become a learning experience for those involved, its salient feature being its dynamic, intercultural aspect;

- permitted discussion on the topics and policies of education and development, which were thus refined and rendered easier to disseminate, creating a multiplier effect.

Appendix II: The foreseeable future of adult education?

While unable here to describe precisely what society will be like 20 years from now, we think we can single out a few features of its development which will influence adult education.

The changing nature of work

From the standpoint of work, it is not particularly bold or original to say that it will be much more technical and that the pace and variety of developments in technology will constantly quicken and increase, so that all adults will have to constantly raise the level of their basic (general and technical) skills.

The nature of work will evolve towards activities increasingly focusing on control, with the related *necessity to "mobilise" one's knowledge very rapidly*. People will have to be more able to react to incidents and difficulties rather than to do things; more able to understand innovation and to innovate than to be able to exercise a function in the traditional meaning of the term. We must discover an education of "reaction" rather than of action, of novelty rather than routine, of the abnormal rather than the normal. It is indeed agents of change that will have to be trained, as much in the interest of the persons concerned as of society, for *the person who is mobile becomes a driving force*.

Another change which has already begun and is likely to become more marked is the change in company structures: dichotomies, such as technology and administration, manual speciality and general training, are tending to disappear; it will no longer be possible for the "lathe operator" of tomorrow to remain ignorant of certain areas of computing, statistics and management.

Changes in "non-working" life

The duration of non-occupational activities will be greater, both during working life — through a reduction in working time — and, beyond that, through longer retirement. Also, long hours of idleness, due to automation for example, will be a feature of working time, though this does not mean that they will be leisure.

The influx (and thus the consumption) of information (political, cultural and educational) will be increasingly diversified and increasingly hard to select and assess. The adult will therefore have greater and greater need of independence, on pain of being alienated by the range of choice.

A mix of educational needs for work and non-work

Will there ultimately still be a discontinuity between the training needs for work and for non-work? ... This hardly seems likely, for the means of taking charge of oneself will be identical, or at any rate similar, in both cases. There is reason to believe that learning to react quickly to a situation will be as much a feature of working life as outside it, and that both will benefit therefrom.

Training social man

These considerations lead to conclusions which nevertheless lack one essential element, namely man as a social being. What has been said prompts us to pursue training of the kind that teaches man to react to his environment, but to react alone. To this must be added training man as a social animal, living in communities, capable of understanding his fellows, of partly sacrificing his own aspirations to those of the community. And the community should be in a position both to express its needs as a com-

munity and to assume responsibility for their development. Far from precluding the possibility of the personal
development of the individuals making up that community, mutual training is, on the contrary, one of its trump
cards. These few pointers on the constraints facing adult
education are admittedly of the present, but they may
conceivably be valid for a long time to come.

Bertrand Schwartz (0/79-81)

Appendix III: Will "school" be able to meet the needs?

"The problem is still awaiting a solution, for the educational system largely operates without concerning itself with the job market, at least for the time being. However, it should immediately be said that educational structures are not and cannot be designed in accordance with the job market. The gulf is already obvious. The system is inappropriate and not adaptable. Schools are national; they serve the interests of linguistic unity and national identity.

These three pillars are now being shaken. The "nation" is wavering between the two superpowers on the one hand and the aggressiveness of regional particularities on the other: linguistic unity is disappearing owing to new ways of thinking and pressures impacting on national languages (superlanguage and dialects). Industrial civilisation seems to be an important factor, but new and different civilisations now stand alongside it, like so many suckers in a neat garden suddenly gone tropical. The fact is that teachers, the purveyors of information, technologies and changing values, strive to be up to date (retraining courses, refresher courses). They often seem like pilots of propeller aircraft entrusted, not with supersonic aircraft but with spacecraft (in other words, "controlled by others").

We also wonder whether it is appropriate to propagate the new computer-based training/education or whether it would be preferable to set our sights on different goals, for in future the bulk of jobs will require increasingly modest skills. Do we not already drive cars without any particular knowledge of internal combustion engines, a sound knowledge of the highway code seeming more important? For example, those who use what the economy produces are calling for the adoption, in upper secondary school, of new subjects such as the nuclear age, international relations, socialism and communism, preparation for parenthood, drug addiction, alcoholism and so on.

The new jobs do not require great skills — perhaps they even require negligible ones — and no one thinks about what kind of values we will have when our tasks are modest and unappealing. Faced with the reality of increasingly automated industries, the Japanese trade unions are demanding that jobs be reserved for their members (and would be satisfied, for example, with any nondescript warehouseman's job for a superfluous engineer); but no one reflects on the cultural and social price of such a change.

Saverio Avveduto (14/38-40)

Appendix IV: Nine major general policy features of Project No. 9

1. Development is above all a policy and strategy that evolve.

2. If development must look to the local level for its origin and point of entry, this does not mean that it is defensive and inward-looking. It supposes a link with wider networks of solidarities.

3. Local and regional development are not decreed from on high, any more than they are born spontaneously.

4. Development calls for the mobilisation of all local resources, material as well as human.

5. Local and regional development must not be reduced to the sum total of the social, economic, cultural, political or ecological dimensions, but must take into account reality, interactions and possibly synergies between its various components as a whole.

6. Development is a process which combines planning, programming and the genius for adapting to unforeseen circumstances.

7. The process of local development is also a process of training, just as training is indissociable from the development of the community.

8. Learning, in the development context, is based on motivation; it is geared to objectives, centred on the learner and on the problems, and does not contain elements which:

    a. characterise the traditional teacher/instructor — pupil relationship;

    b. involve the use of techniques used for transferring the theoretical and practical techniques learned in class and in the workshop to everyday life.

9. Depending on the context in which they are implemented, development projects create new functions and new job profiles. (17/31-33)

Once lack of training had been defined as an obstacle to vocational integration, it was doubtless legitimate to seek responses to unemployment through the development of training facilities.

This action had some effect: in the case of retraining schemes, it helped to delay the onset of unemployment and, in certain cases, to procure additional resources for the unemployed. It also made it possible for some people to maintain or acquire the status of unemployed, which they were not recognised as being before. Lastly, the links created among trainees permitted subsequent retraining in unexpected areas. Overall however, the "training solution" did not succeed in solving unemployment in the way those promoting it hoped.

The training "gaps" are not very easy to define, to pinpoint, and still less to fill. For what are the criteria for defining gaps? For what tasks, what jobs are job-seekers to be prepared? Could skills be defined, and attempts made to impart them through specific training courses corresponding to these new jobs? As all the surveys clearly show, a particular job can be secured via various training routes and similar jobs call for different skills, depending on the forms of organisation and the work supply. Unemployment cannot therefore be reduced to adapting the supply and demand for training.

The structural changes in the working population that will have had a greater effect on the conditions determining the absorption of graduates into jobs. On the one hand, the growth in tertiary employment only partly offsets the reduction in industrial employment and joblessness is rising substantially. There is also a rise in the supply of graduates resulting from the increase in the population of school age. As a result, industry has a greater choice in selecting job applicants.

In this context, recruitment policies in industry will increasingly tend to resort to flexible, external forms of employment. In other words, they will make use of all the opportunities offered by unemployment to match their workforce as closely as possible to the market, using fixed-term contracts, part-time contracts, temporary contracts, sub-contracting etc. (54/46-47)

Appendix V: Project No. 9 — A fertile seam of 14 experiments

Co-operative Development Group No. 1 "Participation of women and men in decisions affecting their daily life on a wide range of local and regional issues"

Switzerland — experiment by the Ligue Romanche (Canton of Grisons): to encourage the population to use the Rhaeto-Romanic language conceived as a socio-geographical entity; the use of a language takes account of cultural specificities, of community awareness likely to lead to the planning and implementation of development measures linked to everyday experience.

Spain (Coria, Estremadura): experimenting with adult training procedures in order to promote a local approach turning cultural specificities to account in order to counteract the effects of urban industrial development.

Portugal (Braga): the launching of an educational planning policy for training/development in a regional context in conjunction with a study on decentralisation. This experiment provides an opportunity for a structural approach (charting the services) based on development objectives and the promotion of local cultural identity.

Italy (Sicily): from a former nursery school converted to an adult training centre, helping adults to adapt to and control the environment and supporting educational efforts aimed at children.

Co-operative Development Group No. 2 "Responses to unemployment and to the consequences of economic restructuring"

Finland (Helsinki, Lahti, Padasjoki and Imatra): revitalising the social fabric through micro-planning, linking employment, housing and adult training; using a fund of research and experimentation for development projects.

Belgium (FUNOC — Training for the Open University of Charleroi): opening up the university to workers, using crash courses or incentive courses, skill updating courses and environment-related training courses; making the training structure into an instrument of social mobilisation for fostering the emergence of a type of development promoted by the disadvantaged.

Sweden (Landskrona): running an "extramural retraining" scheme for the benefit of the former employees of a shipyard using the opportunities provided by the existing educational and financing structures; creating a "meeting centre" (in one of the shipyard sheds); dealing with the traumas caused by the re-evaluation of one particular type of development.

Denmark (Silkeborg): innovatory practices linked to local problems with a view to including disadvantaged groups in a scheme to raise the level of vocational qualifications as well as awareness of community development (training linked to the use of the Danish language, working conditions, living conditions, etc.).

Federal Republic of Germany (Church of Kurhessen Waldeck — Kassel): the development of a project for unemployed youngsters (Treffpunkt); studying all aspects of the changing lifestyles of the young in this period of transition; making connections between "Christian" topics, ideas about the future, the development of enterprise skills (importance of guidance).

France ("Idées Vosges" — Remiremont): liaison in a "devitalised" area to develop local initiatives in designing and implementing projects; providing support during this process to those involved, whether individuals or groups.

Co-operative Development Group No. 3 "Evolution of the social and cultural roles of women and men". Co-ordination of all the organisations in a comprehensive (guidance, training) scheme aimed at sensitive groups. As a response to the crisis, opening up new possibilities by influencing the development of the social and cultural roles of men and women

The Dutch project (Almelo, Enschede, Hengelo): providing training in dealing with marginal groups (especially female immigrants) against a background of the serious employment crisis; co-ordinating the training system to make it more relevant.

United Kingdom (National Federation of Women's Institutes): originally, the purpose of this scheme was to improve the living conditions of women in rural areas (training in health and home economics). But it has now expanded to include the role of women in social life, in the life of their own organisation.

Turkey (Ankara): completion of a network of education centres devoted to identifying the local needs of the population and handling the organisation of communities; integrating public administrative services into a co-operative system based on local demands.

Norway (Tromsø): drawing up a plan for sexual equality; decentralising teacher training at local level to help to ensure that local needs are catered for.

Appendix VI: "Adult education and social change" (1988-93). Declaration of the final conference (Strasbourg, 22-25 March 1993)

Considering:

- Europe's social fabric and its democratic structures to be under threat;
- the steadily worsening employment situation and the resulting difficulties faced by large sections of the population with respect to access to employment;
- the foreseeable demographic changes, which will contribute to an increase in the proportion of elderly people and constitute a decisive challenge to the management of our societies in three age-groups;
- the transformation of social roles, relationships at work, economic, social and political relations, and identity-forming processes, which means that the current generation of adults is particularly vulnerable.

Convinced:

- that democracy must enable each individual to participate fully in determining the choices which will shape his or her destiny, and to play an active role in the development process;
- that adult education is an ideal way of developing the human skills demanded by the challenges of our time, and a powerful means of building and consolidating democracy and the rights of disadvantaged individuals and groups;
- that proposals relating to education are inseparable from more fundamental options for economic, social, political, cultural and local democracy.

Emphasising:

- that there is still much inequality of access and disparity amongst facilities available, despite the unprecedented development of training over the last decades and the general consensus which it enjoys,

The participants at the Conference organised by the Council of Europe on "Adult Education and Social Change in Europe; Development for all" held on 22-25 March 1993 in Strasbourg, having analysed with satisfaction the extremely positive results of activities initiated by the Council of Europe under the umbrella of the project on "Adult education and social change", in which 25 countries participated, notably by funding 39 seminars or study visits.

Declare that:

- vocational training is not the only answer to unemployment;
- the changes in employment and work are having a strong impact on the relationship between general education and vocational training as hitherto defined and are consequently necessitating an adaptation of structures and curricula to reinforce the dialectical links between initial education, adult education and vocational training;
- given the structural nature of the changes under way, any project relating to education must be focused on citizenship and the continuity of the socialisation process of each individual, group or community.

At all levels, it is important to recognise the important role of adult education, as regards its working methods as well as its contents, when building democratic citizenship.

- adult education must be extended to all adults without distinction and a service must be set up to provide individual help and advice on working out options and defining a personalised course of training;

- the education provided must allow the individual to acquire the flexibility and capacity to anticipate which are necessary for active participation in the creation of wealth, knowledge and new cultural values;

- neither initial education nor vocational training alone can fulfil this role;

- the priority task is to create a coherent system out of elements which are currently dissimilar, fragmented and enfeebled, in order to construct an educational system geared to the requirements dictated by the democratic construction of an information-based society;

- political will is the only factor that will allow conversion on a large scale, especially if the effective use of the new communication and information media is envisaged as could be desirable.

To this end, the participants recommend in accordance with the principles of reform set out in the appendix, that member states:

- examine the conditions in which the right to lifelong education might be extended and made available to all adults;

- promote a policy of participation by adults in education through tax exemptions or reductions;

- examine the ways and means for achieving a coherent policy on adult education (framework legislation);

- consider the possibility of co-ordinating the actions of various ministries responsible for adult education;

- enlist the aid of business and industry in the promotion of adult education;

- encourage the formation of an organised, coherent

adult education sector, characterised by efficiency and a diverse range of responses as well as on the industrialisation of its modes of production and distribution;

- envisage the reallocation of funds, taking the possibility of budgetary transfers into account, such reallocation being made with reference to a job related approach;

    a. emancipation contributing to the development of the individual and his or her autonomy, facilitates community involvement and making people more employable;

    b. vocational education and training as a means of boosting employment and contributing to economic restructuring and social change;

- recognise the vital contribution of voluntary organisations and allocate resources to them accordingly.

The participants unanimously urge the Council of Europe to ensure that adult education remains a specific, permanent focal point of its work, as a crucial factor and ideal means of strengthening pluralist democracy and human rights, seeking solutions to the problems facing society, and promoting awareness of a European cultural identity.

The participants recommend that the Council of Europe take the initiative for projects, particularly in the new member states, relating to community involvement and local development, which are factors important to democratisation.

The participants recommend that the Council for Cultural Co-operation, through increased co-operation with the other steering committees:

- take all the necessary steps to strengthen the international network of co-operation and regular exchange of information and experience between member countries;

- examine the value of institutional arrangements for meeting requests for assistance and technical exchanges, particularly from the new member states;
- concentrate the Council of Europe's further work in this field on those educational elements such as the educational role of towns, the contribution of minority groups to the construction of democracy, which might remove barriers to more active citizenship.

The participants recommend that the Council of Europe:

Recognise adult education as a fundamental vector, and as one way of providing the countries of central and eastern Europe with the services necessary for the construction of democratic political regimes and for the gradual participation of ethnic and linguistic minorities in European life;

Define the right of adults to education as part of the extension of the scope of "human rights", but also recognise it as an essential means of giving human rights a tangible form, a means which is as important as formal, legal guarantees;

Examine a suitable form for an instrument setting minimum conditions and criteria to be offered by member states, with the aim of meeting effectively the needs of adult education;

Encourage member states to develop a coherent, integrated policy for adult education;

Publicise this declaration and appendix, and the reference documents on which they are based, as widely as possible among the people and organisations engaged in the various forms of adult education.

Appendix to the draft declaration of the final conference

Any time of change is also a time of choice. The major, complex changes now taking place must be coupled with an intense educational effort and a relearning process for all, if serious political and social regression is to be avoided.

At the present time, millions of men and women acutely need to update their skills in order to cope with the new situations in employment, unemployment and leisure, and generally, the conditions of their socialisation, in general. Societies cannot reject or leave untapped substantial reserves of talent and experience and must primarily concern themselves with the predicament of those that education has left on the sidelines because of their economic situation, because they belong to a minority, because of their sex or a disability. Moreover the cultural trends observed will continue far into the future, bringing opportunities and challenges which will require individuals to show capacities for adaptation and innovation and will entail a permanent learning process and social involvement as never before.

The recognition of the importance and relevance of a coherent, systematically organised policy for adult education must however go hand in hand with its implementation. Although broad sectors of adult education have been converted to the principles of lifelong education, after the years of recession and of coping with its social and vocational consequences, the vocational training sector has come to dominate almost all national systems, without being in a position to meet fully the new needs arising from the "information and communications revolution".

Adult education should make it possible not only to acquire the vocational skills demanded by a rapidly changing labour market, but more generally to:

- satisfy the aspiration of individuals and groups regarding identity and feelings of community;

- change attitudes and develop the particular skills demanded by change;

- bring men and women to an awareness of present-day issues and foster their aptitude to understand and act.

To this end, it is important to reform adult education with the aim of improving its efficiency and charting a course for its future development in line with the following principles:

- recognise adult education as an individual right:

- a right of each adult to embark upon education of good quality throughout life, and irrespective of age, sex, ethnic or linguistic grouping, social, marital or professional status, the presence of disability or the individual's financial situation;

- a right to educational leave, as much for the purpose of broadening general culture as for vocational advancement;

- right of equal access to educational opportunities;

- right to have previous experience assessed and, as appropriate, recognised and validated under official certification arrangements;

- a right to participate or be adequately represented in all phases of the planning, implementation and evaluation of adult education;

- right to have learning facilitated and organised by competent teachers or trainers;

- give training its full place as a preventive measure, including, perhaps with special emphasis on the dimension of general education, thanks to which change can be accomplished more successfully;

- render adult education coherent and homogeneous while allowing it to meet, in diverse ways, the many expectations of a differentiated "clientele", by seeking greater complementarity between general education and vocational training;

- back up the flexibility of educational options with an effective information and guidance system, thus basing the initial commitment to an educational process on genuine "negotiation";

- "knock down the walls" which surround adult education in order to anchor it more firmly in reality;

- open up educational action to professionals other than educationists, thus helping to make a better distinction between training and information;

- recognise that adult education is a partnership involving the whole community (adult learners, organisations, adult teachers/trainers, management and labour, administrations, etc.) and establish structures and networks of participation and decision-making at all levels, in order to boost the development and improve the assessment of adult education facilities;

- secure co-operation at local level between all the educational and culture components and non-educational social services;

- organise functional, co-operative co-ordination between the departments responsible for various aspects of adult education, in order to avoid duplication of effort and to ensure a more realistic distribution of resources, more effective organisation and communication, the dissemination of innovations and the identification of unmet needs;

- develop programmes to enhance the professional status of teachers/trainers and voluntary workers;

- apply the principles of subsidiarity and solidarity at all levels in the formulation of policies and the practical implementation of adult education, in order to co-ordinate the whole, guarantee the protection of minorities, counterbalance inequalities and determine general standards.

It will fall to local authorities, in particular, to:

- recognise that adult education has a role to play in the rethinking of existing patterns of development and that it can facilitate the emergence of new models of developments;

- base the planning and development of training places on negotiations with all concerned;

- contribute to the establishment of educational options which enable learners to enter into and to pursue their education in the best possible conditions, particularly by developing a coherent system of assessment and recognition of achievements.

It will fall to educational organisations in particular to rethink the manner of devising and dispensing education and training, in other words to:

- take the whole person into consideration together with his or her socio-cultural background (global approach) and adapt curricula more closely to local realities and to the ongoing necessity to learn how to learn and to adapt;

- view education as a lifelong process of development, encompassing the entire sweep of people's emotional, physical and intellectual capacities, memory and imagination, sense of individuality and community and their aptitudes to find their bearings, to act, to learn how to learn, etc.;

- provide a range of educational opportunities, relevant to a contemporary social setting (health, family life, pluralism, rights of ethnic minorities, right to a healthy environment, spiritual and personal values, social justice, human rights, unemployment, immigration, illiteracy, poverty, etc. as "way of life");

- set up networks of organisations, in the knowledge that educational establishments are not the only places where people learn, but that they are the only places where experience is systematically reviewed for the purpose of formalising it;

- aim for a modular approach and curricula established in terms of "units/credits", seek to have educational sequences based on continuums offering learners considerable flexibility of options;

- make all adult learners equally welcome, and set up a service of assistance and advice tailored to the individual, for the purpose of helping learners to construct a project and to negotiate a suitable course of learning;

- guarantee quality in curricula and services;

- facilitate access by all adults, by offering various services, especially child-minding centres and transport;

- set up committees at different levels, thus charting a course for adult education on the basis of the concerns of a widely represented environment, and not purely the arguments of teachers/trainers;

- define a minimum level of skills and qualifications for adult teachers/trainers, broaden their status, encourage the development of career structures and enhance the professional status of staff (whether or not on a pay-roll) by promoting training (modular, co-ordinated and certified training) for all categories of adult teachers/trainers;

- make assessment a regular dimension of adult education projects.

For giving him the opportunity to work on these topics alongside the Council of Europe's Directorate of Education, Culture and Sport, and for their kindly guidance, the author would like to express his sincere gratitude to Mr Raymond Weber and Mr Maitland Stobart. Mrs Maura Rolandi-Ricci and Mr Jean-Pierre Titz will recognise here the testimony of my gratitude for their demanding friendship. Mr Mehmet Önat will hear echoes of shared convictions. The members of the Steering Group and working groups will, we hope, find our lively and protracted discussions reflected in these pages.

Sales agents for publications of the Council of Europe
Agents de vente des publications du Conseil de l'Europe

AUSTRALIA/AUSTRALIE
Hunter Publications, 58A, Gipps Street
AUS-3066 COLLINGWOOD, Victoria

AUSTRIA/AUTRICHE
Gerold und Co., Graben 31
A-1011 WIEN 1

BELGIUM/BELGIQUE
La Librairie européenne SA
50, avenue A. Jonnart
B-1200 BRUXELLES 20

Jean de Lannoy
202, avenue du Roi
B-1060 BRUXELLES

CANADA
Renouf Publishing Company Limited
1294 Algoma Road
CDN-OTTAWA ONT K1B 3W8

CYPRUS/CHYPRE
MAM
The House of the Cyprus Book
PO Box 1722, CY-NICOSIA

DENMARK/DANEMARK
Munksgaard
Book and Subscription Service
PO Box 2148
DK-1016 KØBENHAVN K

FINLAND/FINLANDE
Akateeminen Kirjakauppa
Keskuskatu 1, PO Box 218
SF-00381 HELSINKI

GERMANY/ALLEMAGNE
UNO Verlag
Poppelsdorfer Allee 55
D-53115 BONN

GREECE/GRÈCE
Librairie Kauffmann
Mavrokordatou 9, GR-ATHINAI 106 78

IRELAND/IRLANDE
Government Stationery Office
Publications Section
4-5 Harcourt Road, IRL-DUBLIN 2

ISRAEL/ISRAËL
ROY International
PO Box 13056
IL-61130 TEL AVIV

ITALY/ITALIE
Libreria Commissionaria Sansoni
Via Duca di Calabria, 1/1
Casella Postale 552, I-50125 FIRENZE

LUXEMBOURG
Librairie Bourbon
(Imprimerie Saint-Paul)
11, rue Bourbon
L-1249 LUXEMBOURG

NETHERLANDS/PAYS-BAS
InOr-publikaties, PO Box 202
NL-7480 AE HAAKSBERGEN

NORWAY/NORVÈGE
Akademika, A/S Universitetsbokhandel
PO Box 84, Blindern
N-0314 OSLO

PORTUGAL
Livraria Portugal, Rua do Carmo, 70
P-1200 LISBOA

SPAIN/ ESPAGNE
Mundi-Prensa Libros SA
Castelló 37, E-28001 MADRID

Llibreria de la Generalitat
Rambla dels Estudis, 118
E-08002 BARCELONA

Llibreria de la Generalitat de Catalunya
Gran Via Jaume I, 38, E-17001 GIRONA

SWEDEN/SUÈDE
Aktiebolaget CE Fritzes
Regeringsgatan 12, Box 163 56
S-10327 STOCKHOLM

SWITZERLAND/SUISSE
Buchhandlung Heinimann & Co.
Kirchgasse 17, CH-8001 ZÜRICH

BERSY
Route du Manège 60
CP 4040
CH-1950 SION 4

TURKEY/TURQUIE
Yab-Yay Yayimcilik Sanayi Dagitim Tic Ltd
Barbaros Bulvari 61 Kat 3 Daire 3
Besiktas, TR-ISTANBUL

UNITED KINGDOM/ROYAUME-UNI
HMSO, Agency Section
51 Nine Elms Lane
GB-LONDON SW8 5DR

**UNITED STATES and CANADA/
ÉTATS-UNIS et CANADA**
Manhattan Publishing Company
468 Albany Post Road
PO Box 850
CROTON-ON-HUDSON, NY 10520

STRASBOURG
Librairie internationale Kléber
1, rue des Francs-Bourgeois
F-67000 STRASBOURG

Librairie des Facultés
2-12, rue de Rome
F-67000 STRASBOURG

Librairie Kléber
Palais de l'Europe
F-67075 STRASBOURG Cedex

Council of Europe Press/Les éditions du Conseil de l'Europe
Council of Europe/Conseil de l'Europe
F-67075 Strasbourg Cedex